Richard Milton was born in London in journalist and broadcaster since 1968. In journalism, he has reported on many hundreds of britains companies and interviewed their senior executives. In *Bad Company*, Milton tells the stories that didn't get published, and uses a unique new insight into corporate personality to analyse dozens of cases of corporate bad behaviour.

Milton's previous books, *Alternative Science* and *Shattering the Myths of Darwinism*, sparked heated controversy in the scientific and academic communities. In addition to a growing list of successful non-fiction books, Richard Milton's first novel, *Dead Secret*, was recently published by House of Stratus. To read excerpts, visit www.DeadSecret.com

BAD
COMPANY
BEHIND THE CORPORATE MASK

RICHARD MILTON

HOUSE OF
STRATUS

This edition published in 2001 by House of Stratus, an imprint of Stratus Holdings plc, 24c Old Burlington Street, London, W1X 1RL, UK. Also at: Suite 210, 1270 Avenue of the Americas, New York, NY 10020, USA.

www.houseofstratus.com

Typeset, printed and bound by House of Stratus.

A catalogue record for this book is available from the British Library and the Library of Congress.

ISBN 0-7551-0151-0

'It is better to be alone than in bad company'
George Washington (1732–99)

CONTENTS

CHAPTER ONE

JEKYLL AND HYDE PLC
How the corporate mind works...*and how Shell sank its corporate image*

Imagine you're responsible for running one of the world's biggest oil companies that has for many decades nurtured an enviable reputation as the motorist's friend. Imagine that you stand each morning at your office window, gazing down from your tower block with quiet pride at the hundreds of motorists pulling into your brightly-lit, clean, friendly service stations to spend money filling up at your pumps, rather than those of your competitors: a scene repeated daily by millions of motorists around the world.

Now imagine that you tow your friendly, caring corporate image out into the north Atlantic and sink it into oblivion, a thousand fathoms down to the bottom of the ocean.

This may sound like a corporate nightmare, but it was exactly what happened to Shell in 1995 when it planned to dump its Brent Spar oil platform, with many tons of toxic waste, by sinking it at sea. The plan sparked a Europe-wide boycott of Shell stations by its customers, which cost the company millions of pounds in lost revenue and forced it to change its policy.

What on earth can have induced a major corporation like Shell, Europe's largest company, a pillar of the commercial establishment, to tear up twenty-five years of investment in projects to protect the environment and behave instead like an environmental Jack the Ripper?

The answer to that deceptively innocent question is the subject of this book. The explanation involves a new insight into companies that I

1

believe may, in time, transform all our relationships with the many large corporations that have such a significant effect on our lives. An insight that transfers power back where it belongs – with us, the consumers.

Companies are like people. Like people, companies can enter into contracts, buy and sell property, make charitable donations, award prizes and even erect memorials to themselves in case we forget about them.

Like people, too, companies can be motivated by the entire range of human feelings and human failings: anger, jealousy, greed, incompetence, and fear – fear of failure, fear of disgrace, fear of discovery.

In the 1950s, companies made the astounding discovery that we – their customers – are motivated by feelings quite different from those of which we are consciously aware. The research of depth psychology into buying behaviour uncovered the unexpected fact that when people buy cars or coffee or cake-mix in the high street, they are motivated by unconscious emotions that they are scarcely aware of at all, and that their real motives are sometimes the very opposite of what they consciously believe.

This book approaches corporate behaviour from the same premise: that – just like people – corporations often act from motives of which they are scarcely consciously aware. That just like their customers, companies' motives are not what their managers believe and say they are, but often spring unbidden from concealed and dark recesses in the corporate psyche.

Bad Company puts some of the world's largest and best-known corporations on the analyst's couch, to find out what their unconscious motivations are and how those unconscious emotions have resulted in otherwise inexplicable behaviour – even apparently insane behaviour – in the recent past.

Take Coca-Cola, for example. In 1985, the company was the world's largest soft drink vendor with the greatest daily sale of the most famous brand name on Earth. The corporation's entire fortune and market goodwill were founded on just one thing: the taste of Coke. Yet, at the peak of its success, the company arbitrarily decided to change that taste and re-launch the product. When, unsurprisingly, customers said they did not like the new taste, Coca-Cola was compelled to contrive an expensive and humiliating retreat back to the old established flavour. Anyone can make a mistake; but what exactly led Coca-Cola to believe it could arbitrarily impose a new brand on its customers around the world without provoking dissent? Even more fascinating, whatever possessed it to risk the whole company on such a mad gamble?

Coke and Shell are far from alone in suddenly lurching away from the restraints of reasoned and temperate behaviour into a course of action that, in any human individual, we would regard as at best eccentric, at worst, certifiable.

Intel Corporation owns more than 80 per cent of the world market for computer chips and built its reputation on the precision of its products. In 1994, Intel launched its Pentium chip, but found that there was a tiny error in the design, resulting in it getting its sums slightly wrong. Intel tried to ignore the growing clamour of its customers for months, refusing to replace the faulty chips and insisting that nothing was amiss – until customer pressure compelled it to relent at a cost of hundreds of millions of dollars. Why did Intel bury its head in the sand when its reputation for precision – and its credibility – was crucially at risk?

Hamburger chain McDonald's decided to sue for libel two vegetarian protesters, who no one had ever heard of, for handing out critical leaflets outside its restaurants. As a result the company became bogged down in a two-year-long nightmare of worldwide bad publicity and public humiliation as the unemployed defendants washed McDonald's dirty linen in public. Why did the world's biggest restaurant chain, richer than many a small country, resort to litigation and jeopardise literally billions of dollars spent on marketing and advertising over decades?

Italian casual clothing manufacturer, Benetton, conceived an advertising campaign based on images of human suffering and death that was widely condemned in countries all over Europe, that caused thousands of customers to boycott its shops, and even caused some of its *own* retail outlets to sue for loss of earnings. What compelled one of Europe's leading corporations to casually point a pistol to its head and play a game of corporate Russian roulette?

Dozens more examples of a similar kind are analysed in detail in later chapters, pointing to a malady that is common to many large organisations. Often this kind of behaviour by companies is simply written off as a mistake, a failure of management or of product or market research. Sometimes a deeper cause is suspected – that actions like Shell's or Coca Cola's stem from corporate arrogance; that companies are so wealthy and so powerful that they feel free to behave as they wish, regardless of the rights or feelings of others. Yet even a casual inspection of these suggested causes shows that they cannot be a complete explanation. No one, however arrogant, or however mistaken, deliberately places a gun to their head and pulls the trigger: the motivations we are seeking are profoundly self-destructive and are buried far more deeply in the corporate psyche.

To see incidents like these simply as a failure of management, as 'pilot error' on the part of the chief executive and his or her colleagues, is to mistake the nature of these episodes fundamentally. In each of the cases mentioned above, and the many others examined later, it was not the isolated decisions of one or a few misguided individuals that determined the corporation's behaviour; it was the natural thoughts and feelings of many individuals acting in concert, obeying a deep corporate impulse that expressed a fundamental feature of the company's personality: its way of doing business; its outlook on the world; its *style*. It was the real organisation briefly revealing itself from behind the corporate mask. Even actions like Shell's and Coca-Cola's make perfect sense once you understand the unconscious logic that underlies them. And, more importantly, once you understand them, you can deal with them on equal terms.

To say that companies have a personality is more than merely a metaphor. I am not simply comparing the behaviour of companies with that of individuals and drawing anthropomorphic conclusions, like Beatrix Potter fitting out Benjamin Bunny with a suit of Sunday clothes. The idea of a corporate mind and a corporate unconscious is a model taken from experimental psychology that accords with the findings of extensive academic research into the dynamics of groups and organisations; of the type of personality most likely to be attracted to, and most likely to thrive in, the corporate environment and of the evolution of a group personality in such organisations.

From the point of view of interpreting their behaviour, there is one very important way in which companies are directly comparable to individuals. In general, people who are emotionally distressed exhibit disturbances in their outward behaviour. At the same time, it is a peculiarity of people who are neurotic or psychotic that the things they say often appear perfectly rational, and seem to make perfect sense. This is usually because the person has unconsciously constructed a verbal, rational explanation as a façade to mask or excuse their abnormal behaviour. For this reason, professional psychotherapists pay less attention to what their patients say and more to what they actually do. If a neurotic person compulsively washes his hands dozens of times a day, for example, that behaviour will be taken as a more reliable outward sign of some inner disturbance than his or her claim to be simply worried about hygiene.

In this respect, as in many others, companies are just like people. The things that companies do, and the rationalisations they offer for their behaviour, are often very revealing of what is really going on in the corporate unconscious. Companies may resist the true explanation of their behaviour just as a neurotic patient resists the psychotherapist's interpretations of his disturbance; but the more a patient seeks to conceal his true motivations, the more he reveals.

In the decades before the advent of psychoanalytic techniques and of depth psychology, a useful metaphor for the contrast between the individual's outward behaviour and the turbulent, disguised inner life was Robert Louis Stevenson's famous tale of Doctor Jekyll and Mister Hyde. Stevenson conceived this seminal story because of sensational real events that had occurred in Edinburgh a century earlier, concerning Deacon Brodie, a highly respected Edinburgh family man, town councillor and pillar of the church. Edinburgh had been plagued by a gang of burglars and the whole city was on edge. When police finally netted the villains, and unmasked the head of their gang, he turned out to be none other than the worthy Deacon who, it seemed, was law-abiding and respectable only by day, but by night was a demonic burglar.

The 'double life' theme fascinated Stevenson and eventually became the famous story of the respectable doctor who gains access to the evil side of his personality through a drug that he concocts.

What is perhaps most shocking to us about the transformation of the fictional Henry Jekyll into the amoral Mister Hyde is that, as a medical man, he is obliged by professional duty and by law to remain always morally correct and to respect his fellow man. He is never permitted, like the rest of us, to stumble occasionally, or ever to give way to any darker impulse. Jekyll has to be *more* responsible, not less.

The Jekyll and Hyde metaphor is no less useful in understanding the contrast between the outward behaviour of organisations and their unconscious motivations. Like the decent Jekyll, corporations are always on duty under public scrutiny and must remain always honest, just, courteous and helpful. Ford, IBM, Shell, McDonald's and all the others may never snarl an insult, may never kick the cat – never behave badly, whatever the provocation, whatever the circumstances. Not surprisingly, there is an unconscious price to be paid for this unnaturally angelic mask. It isn't only deacons of the church who can turn into burglars and sociopaths in the dead of night.

How Shell Sank its Corporate Image

Oil has been extracted from the North Sea for more than 30 years, and the cold, grey waters around Scotland have become littered with hundreds of oil platforms, many nearing the end of their operational life. The very oldest are now unwanted, rusting hulks: a forlorn end to decades of loyal service.

Even the most calloused roughneck of the rigs must have felt a twinge of regret when, in 1995, Shell UK announced that it was to dispose of one of the longest-serving installations, the 14,500-ton Brent Spar storage platform. But if anyone on land or sea felt such nostalgia, it must have been rapidly swept away by Shell's announcement regarding how they planned to dispose of it. Shell had sought permission from the British government to tow Brent Spar out into the Atlantic Ocean and simply sink it at sea.

Shell's experts had done a study of the problem and had concluded that deep-sea disposal was the best option for five reasons: that other methods of disposal, such as dismantling on land, were technically complex; that deep sea disposal greatly reduced the risk to the people involved; that it offered 'negligible environmental disadvantage'; that it was the 'lowest cost option'; and that it was 'acceptable to the authorities and their consultees'.[1]

Put simply, Shell had decided on disposal at sea because, the company said, that was the simplest, safest, cheapest, least damaging option and one that everyone who mattered was happy with.

From the outset, it seemed that money was the major consideration, since Shell's experts estimated that to take the Brent Spar back on land and scrap it would cost around £45 million, whereas disposal at sea would cost only £11 million. On the face of it, the issue was principally a financial one, and hence they made a purely rational decision. It was this issue more than any other that, later on, cast doubt on whether Shell really was acting rationally or from some unconscious, irrational motive.

When Shell's plan became public, it aroused a storm of protest from environmentalists who said that disposing of Brent Spar at sea would be a major source of pollution. Environmental organisation, Greenpeace, published a report on the decommissioning and abandonment of offshore oil platforms, in which it pointed out that the dumping could set a precedent for disposal of the other 400 North Sea oil rigs. The report concluded that total removal of Brent Spar was 'not only cost-effective, feasible and job-saving, but the best environmental option'.[2]

According to Greenpeace, Brent Spar contained more than 100 tonnes of hazardous materials including waste oil, heavy metals such as cadmium and arsenic and 30 tonnes of low-level radioactive scale, as well as many tons of oil sludge. Many of these materials would not break down on the seabed; they would accumulate in the bodies of marine wildlife. The rusting rig would itself also present a hazard to fishermen and other sea users.

Greenpeace mounted another of the high profile media campaigns for which it has become well known, by occupying the platform for some weeks, before being ejected by Shell security personnel in the now customary confrontation for the TV cameras. Greenpeace also sought to challenge the legality of the dumping in the courts, but the Government employed a procedural manoeuvre that denied Greenpeace access to the courts and what might well have proved an embarrassing and protracted lawsuit.

With its direct action and legal challenges failing to alter Shell's mind, and the date of the proposed sinking rapidly approaching, Greenpeace played its only remaining card: an emotional public appeal. With only weeks to go, it called on motorists throughout Europe to boycott Shell stations when they bought fuel. According to Greenpeace UK's chief campaigner, Chris Rose: 'We had a pretty good idea that the public would see it in clear, simple terms of responsibility. Why, if you can't dump your car in the village pond, is this huge company able to dump its rubbish in your sea?'

To everyone's astonishment, the boycott worked within a matter of days. Its effectiveness varied from country to country: motorists in Germany responding most of all, with Holland, Sweden and Denmark following and Britain itself some way behind. But the cumulative effect on Shell's income was devastating and in a very short space of time amounted to millions of pounds in lost revenue. In Germany, where the boycott was most effective, Shell forecourt sales were reported to have dropped by 30 per cent.

It was in Germany, too, that Greenpeace achieved its first political breakthrough when the German environment minister announced a formal request to Great Britain not to dump Brent Spar. Chancellor Helmut Kohl also applied pressure to Prime Minister John Major over the affair.

It wasn't just the Government in Germany that was opposed to the plan. The general manager of Shell's German subsidiary, Peter Duncan, gave a television interview that was not broadcast at the time but was shown by BBC TV in a documentary the following year. Duncan told the cameras: 'It was quite clear that all those concerned in this decision had wildly underestimated the political implications and [had] an inability to communicate to people what is the logic behind that.'[3]

Not long afterwards, the depth of feeling in Germany was made even clearer when eco-terrorists shot at one Shell station and fire-bombed another.

But it was not terrorist fire-bombs, nor the appeal of Chancellor Helmut Kohl, nor the warnings of the member countries that had signed the Oslo Commission's ban on dumping at sea, which deterred Shell from dumping Brent Spar. It was not even when the president of Shell Netherlands, Jan Slechte, publicly distanced himself from the plan on Dutch TV. It was Shell's own customers who made the company think again. A 30 per cent drop in revenue is unsustainable.

The day before it was due to sink the platform, Shell lost its nerve and made a brief announcement that it had 'decided to abandon deepwater disposal and seek from the UK authorities a license for onshore disposal'.

Shell UK's chairman, Dr Chris Fay, was visibly tight-lipped and angry when he appeared on TV news programmes to confirm the decision and made an almost emotional appeal concerning the difficult position in which his company had been placed. Dr Fay spoke of not knowing where Brent Spar would next rest at anchor in the moving tones usually reserved for people rather than oil rigs.

In a later BBC TV documentary on the affair, Chris Fay described his feelings and those of his colleagues at the time: 'It was very emotional. I think I am blessed with some great staff and they were very supportive. I have to say – that a tear came to the eye is probably an understatement.'[4]

A further clue to Shell's state of mind at this time comes from its director of public affairs, John Whybrew, who said: 'What Greenpeace did was to create a catalyst which in many parts of continental Europe, in Germany but also in Denmark, Sweden, Holland and elsewhere, made people confronted with the campaign become emotionally disturbed.'[5]

So Shell's perception of events was that while its own behaviour was rational – despite the tears that came to its management's eyes at being

9

prevented from dumping Brent Spar – the behaviour of its own customers was 'emotionally disturbed'.

It is important to appreciate that Shell's intention was not frustrated by the antics of environmentalists occupying the platform for the benefit of the TV cameras, not by legal challenges and not by scientific debate, but by economic pressure from its *own customers* – the only people able to mount a boycott.

It is true that environmental organisations, such as Greenpeace and Friends of the Earth, got themselves into high gear to combat Shell's plan and deployed all their media communications skills very effectively. But there was no mass direct-mail campaign to mobilise public support and cash until *after* the plan was defeated. The mass support for a boycott of Shell's pumps that resulted in lost millions was simply there, waiting to be tapped, as soon as the news hit the headlines.

Perhaps most important of all, the public did not need to grow beards, wear sandals or beads and walk the streets with placards to express disapproval. All they had to do was drive a matter of yards further than usual and fill up with fuel from BP, Esso or Texaco – and that was just what they did in their millions in Britain, Germany, Sweden, Denmark, Holland and elsewhere. No one except Shell knows exactly how much the boycott cost in cold cash, but the final total was many millions.

Had Shell possessed a record as an indiscriminate polluter or as careless of environmental issues, then the Brent Spar affair might have made sense as merely another piece of brute insensitivity by yet another anti-social multinational company.

But the most incomprehensible aspect of the whole affair was that Shell has been very active in supporting environmental issues for decades precisely because, as an oil company, it is vulnerable to accusations of pollution. The company has invested large amounts of both cash and hard work and, ironically, 1995 was to be the celebration of the twenty-fifth anniversary of the Better Britain Award, which Shell sponsors.

Had anyone consulted the environmentalists in Shell who have worked so hard for so long to keep the company's image clean, there can be little doubt that they must have been horrified at the implications.

Unfortunately, the decision was taken at a higher level, ostensibly as a matter of operational financial policy, and no one at senior level sought to maintain a consistency between the two policies. The result was that twenty-five years of hard work was thrown away virtually overnight.

Shell approached the Brent Spar issue as if it were an old-style PR problem from the 1980s. It underestimated the popular support its opponents enjoyed. Indeed, it failed entirely to perceive what is obvious with the benefit of hindsight, that its opponents included a large fraction of its own customers.

It acted as though no one would remember, or perhaps that no one would care, that the oil companies had promised the government they would clean up after themselves back in the 1960s when the licenses to drill were being handed out. It produced a stack of convincing-sounding scientific analyses, which appeared to prove its case. It produced another stack of convincing-sounding financial arguments that appeared to prove that decommissioning on land would cost £45 million and hence was out of the question.

But these moves, which were right ten or twenty years ago, failed to work. This failure was partly because people are better informed and partly because they are no longer willing to be fobbed off by companies making cosmetic attempts to appear green while causing large-scale environmental damage.

Shell's crucial mistake, though, was to lose its own public credibility at an early stage in the debate. Shell's claim that dumping a 14,500-tonne oil platform containing toxic waste offered 'negligible environmental disadvantage' was simply an incredible statement and one that was rejected by the majority of informed people, whether environmentalists or not.

It was a simple matter for Greenpeace to claim that Shell had underestimated the environmental impact of the dumping and overestimated the cost of alternative disposal simply as a cynical PR exercise. From that moment on, many people stopped believing any further statements that Shell made, and became receptive to Greenpeace's point of view.

Above all, though, Shell's ostensible reason for dumping at sea – the prohibitive cost of alternative disposal – was blown completely out of the water by the Greenpeace campaign. In June 1995, Greenpeace leaked a copy of a Shell report that had been produced by Dutch salvage company Smit Engineering BV in 1992, showing that the Brent Spar could be towed back to land and decommissioned for only £10 million – £35 million less than the amount Shell claimed in its original estimates and its submission to the government – and even £1 million less than the cost of simply sinking it. The government and the public had been misled. Disposal at sea was not the cheapest option after all.[6]

Shortly after, the *Daily Mirror* discovered a second Dutch company, HeereMac, which said it could do the job for just £19 million – still £26 million less than the amount Shell claimed it would cost. To make matters worse, HeereMac had quoted this price to Shell more than a year earlier. A spokesman said: 'We are amazed at the £45 million being suggested by Shell to dispose of the Spar on land. We quoted around £19 million to do the job, although dismantling is about four times as expensive as sinking. The amounts mentioned in the press bear no relation to our original offer.'

The company said it had also made a second offer to dismantle the platform 'near shore whereby the radioactive waste would be transported and stored in a responsible manner'. HeereMac said it believed there were 'no environmental, safety or economic reasons to dispose of redundant platforms other than onshore'.

The key question in all this is: what on earth made Shell imagine that anyone would accept statements that were fundamentally incredible? What made the company see itself as a source of information so authoritative in relation to us, its customers, that it felt free to behave as it wished – even like Mister Hyde, stalking the streets at night in search of mischief and free of any rational restraint?

On the face of it, the answer is that the company had simply fallen victim to corporate arrogance: it had got away with doing as it liked in the North Sea for 30 years, with successive governments falling over themselves to be compliant with its wishes, and it simply assumed it could continue to do as it wished.

This may well be part of the answer but not the important part. The key to reading Shell's behaviour lies in understanding how large companies like Shell see us, their customers, and how this perception shapes their world view and their actions.

CHAPTER TWO

FIGURES IN A LANDSCAPE
How companies see their customers...*and how Coca-Cola changed the taste of Coke*

Look around the corporate landscape in 2001 and, on the surface, it seems very much like that of twenty years ago. But, just as the city streets have been invisibly plumbed by a network of high-bandwidth fibre-optic cables, so the business environment has been imperceptibly altered beneath the surface: it is the unseen things in the corporate landscape that have changed.

Marshall McLuhan's 'Global Village' is no mere metaphor for today's electronic age: it is a shrewdly precise description of a global thirst for intimate knowledge, by and of everyone on the planet, coupled with a cheap mechanism that delivers such planet-wide access. Because of our insatiable thirst for gossip and the efficiency of the American press, we can know practically every detail of the business dealings of the most powerful man in the world, the President of the US. In the past, such intelligence was available only to the wealthy and powerful. Now it can be accessed through every teenager's games computer.

Every chief executive today pays lip-service to the Internet – the Information Superhighway to which an estimated 100 million users now have access – but I suspect that less than one in ten has sat down at a screen and taken their first faltering step into the strange new world of cyberspace for themselves. If they did, many of them would be profoundly shocked at the easy availability of information of a kind that even five or ten years ago was to be found only in the drawers of top-secret filing cabinets of the world's largest organisations.

The reason is simply that inside every large corporation there are people who believe that if their organisation does something wrong, it deserves to be exposed. They express this belief by handing or emailing documents to activists outside the organisation. Today, all such activists have contacts with the Internet and will publish the documents electronically. This kind of publishing is beyond any practical form of censorship or policing and has even – so far – proved immune to existing laws such as copyright and libel.

More than any other single cause, it is the easy availability of information that has made it impossible for companies like Shell to get away with environmental hooliganism.

Tony Juniper is campaigns manager of environmentalist group Friends of the Earth. Juniper told me, 'The traditional public relations approach has led companies to believe they can manage these kinds of problem in the short term by the kind of control of the message which they were used to in the past.

'They would put a press release out, and it would get printed; they would invite the key constituencies around to a dinner – MPs, peer companies, media – and it would get reported. But the age of public relations has now gone. It's all over. The age of mass communications is now with us, where people are keyed into international computer networks where journalists, politicians and everybody is getting information from all sorts of different sources, not just from the public relations machinery of the large companies. And it's easy to expose them – there's very often nothing they can do about it.'

When, thirty years ago, Distillers Company found out that the Insight team of the *Sunday Times* was planning to write a story about the tragic side-effects of its drug, Thalidomide, it went to court and obtained an injunction preventing the newspaper from writing about the subject.[1] How would a present-day Distillers Company prevent Joe User, or Jo User, from entering details of drug side-effects into their home computer and broadcasting them anonymously worldwide over the Net?

Many of the examples of corporate Russian roulette examined in this book (see Chapter Five for instance) concern the Internet directly. When the improbably named Professor Nicely discovered that there was something wrong with the design of Intel's Pentium computer chip, he did not write a paper for a learned journal or pen a letter to national newspapers. He simply posted an email message on the Internet. When Intel's chief executive, Andy Groves, wanted to respond to his company's critics and reassure his millions of users, once again it was the medium of the Internet to which he turned.

Of course, this particular example concerns an Information Technology corporation, at home in such a medium, and it is less easy to envisage comparable exchanges over the Internet in industries like petrochemicals or fast food. Yet it was through the Internet that Shell's plans for the Brent Spar were made public, and through the Internet that the world learned of the McDonald's libel case.

In 1991, IBM chairman John Akers gave his senior staff a rare tongue-lashing. Formerly the most profitable company in the world, IBM was losing more than $7 million a day and was heading for financial disaster. Akers told his fellow directors: 'The fact that we're losing market share makes me goddam mad... Everyone is too comfortable when the business is in crisis.'[2]

Akers intended his remarks to be confidential but one of the executives present felt that the message was of sufficient importance to share with his own staff. He distributed a memo via IBM's internal electronic mail – forgetting that today there are no limits to the Internet. Within minutes every news service in the world had the message, and knew that IBM's business was in trouble.

The real point here is that the single most important way in which the corporate environment has changed in the past twenty years is in terms of the accessibility of information – corporate information that was previously regarded as sacrosanct.

There are no longer such things as corporate secrets. Companies must assume as a matter of routine that everything they say and do will sooner or later become public knowledge, and act accordingly. For good or ill, companies now inhabit what the late James Goldsmith contemptuously called the 'see-through society'.

The implication of the transparent society for corporations who must manage their relationship with the community is that all the traditional passive forms of reaction to external threat – silence, cover-ups or evasion – are no longer effective options.

In a wired world, where the free flow of information is normal, silence is suspicious.

It is hardly surprising that companies feel beleaguered and bewildered by the dramatic changes in their environment. Twenty years ago, most companies had only three key constituencies or stakeholders to keep happy: the shareholders, the employees, and the City. There were a few minority interests to be looked after but these had little more than nuisance value. The press had to be squared once in a while so that it could be used to communicate the corporate message to those that mattered. Drinks and canapés had to be served to MPs occasionally to ensure they were on-side when regulatory legislation was threatening. Customers were 'a factor in our thinking' and consumerism was beginning to make itself felt as angry voices were raised in the normally church-like silence of the Annual General Meeting. But it was principally in demanding more information, biodegradable packaging, more accountability, greater social responsibility – things that were not too difficult to promise or expensive to concede.

What has increased corporate paranoia today has to do primarily with how the number of stakeholders has expanded to include the press itself, not merely as an instrument of communication, but as a constituency in its own right and, more importantly, to include us – the customers. No longer passive buying units, marketing fodder to be manipulated by the hidden persuaders of advertising and marched meekly through the turnstiles; but truculent, opinionated, contrary, informed, wilful and – worst of all – people with disposable income.

There's nothing new in consumerism itself, of course. It's more than three decades since Ralph Nader and his followers mounted publicity campaigns that compelled General Motors and Ford to change the design of their cars to reflect greater concern with road safety.[3] But consumerism today is very different from consumerism in the 1970s or even the 1980s; different in terms of the numbers of people willing to take action to express disapproval of a company's policies; different in terms of who those people are; and above all, different in terms of how spontaneously they respond to media coverage. Today, Ralph Nader is not merely protesting with placards, he is a candidate for the Presidency of the US – and garnering significant numbers of votes.

In the 1970s, Greenpeace and Friends of the Earth were perceived as a small bunch of well-meaning but slightly eccentric individuals, willing to make a nuisance of themselves in a cause that seemed a little cranky to many people. Those holding the placards and marching in protest were looked on as misfits and malcontents. To make any impression on large corporations, these people had to be dedicated activists, well organised and deploying substantial machinery of communications to mobilise and direct their supporters.

Thirty years on, their protests seem a lot less eccentric. There has been a dramatic increase in the number of children and adults in developed countries suffering from asthma, male fertility is dropping alarmingly, and one in three people in Britain will be affected by cancer. The majority of households have been touched by maladies such as these, which are widely perceived as caused by, or made worse by, environmental pollution. Today, we are all friends of the earth, whether or not we pay our subscriptions and march with placards.

In retrospect, the protesters of the 1970s appear to be not so much malcontents and cranks as far-sighted early adopters of an important new policy, which many informed people now endorse. And companies who opposed or obstructed them come across as short-sighted, reactionary and selfish.

Radio and television weather bulletins now routinely carry warnings of air pollution in cities; the European Commission publishes league tables of pollution on Europe's beaches; the World Health Organisation warns that diseases once thought conquered, like tuberculosis, are now epidemic again – not in the third world, but in developed countries including Britain and the United States. The twin spectres of global warming and depletion of the ozone layer, with increased incidence of skin cancer, haunt the headlines.

People's minds are sensitised to environmental issues just as asthma victims are sensitised to pollution.

The build-up of people's frustration and resentment finds its expression in incidents such as the public reaction to Shell's plan to dump the Brent Spar oil platform in the Atlantic. The mass support for a boycott of Shell's pumps that resulted in lost millions was simply there, waiting to be tapped, as soon as the news hit the headlines.

It isn't just consumers who have started having opinions of their own. The content of most popular magazines and newspapers today, as well as a sizeable number of broadcast programmes, is heavily consumer-oriented. When we read our papers and watch television, we want to hear about products that failed and services that don't live up to expectations, so we can congratulate ourselves on being smart enough to have avoided them and see the guilty companies publicly exposed.

The popular image of journalists toadying to the whims of their powerful proprietor is a misunderstanding of where the real power lies: just as with any other vendor, newspaper editors have to give the customers what they want, or their papers go unsold and their 'power' evaporates. What you and I want in our newspapers is investigation, comparison, disclosure; we want the facts sniffed out and delivered to our door every morning for a few pence. The biggest single target group for this treatment is commercial and industrial companies: the 'fat cats' of the public utilities; the rapacious barons of oil and gas and coal; the penny-pinching chain stores of the high street – all the old stand-bys of tabloid journalism are now also meat for *The Times*, the *Independent* and even the *Daily Telegraph*.

The difference between the press today and the press of twenty years ago is not in how it reports the news. That is still circumscribed by the need to report both sides, to remain neutral and to refrain from editorial comment, as well as kept in check by the laws of libel. What has changed is the selection of news to cover. Twenty years ago, the fact that a motley collection of people had gathered at the docks to protest against the shipping of live animals would have had little news value for most British national newspapers and the broadcast media. It would have been dismissed as 'single issue politics'. Today it is front-page news. Whatever is important to the press has become important to the organisations that the press writes about.

It is perhaps surprising that, despite this increase in the number and variety of forces that have sprung up to scrutinise and challenge the large corporation, many companies actually feel something like contempt for their customers.

Every chief executive will leap up at once to deny that he or she could ever harbour such base feelings. The truth is that it is all too common when the money is rolling in, day in, day out, for the company to look on its customers as unreflecting, undiscriminating individuals who are acting in a largely automatic way, or are innocently buying an unreal image, when they buy fuel, tomatoes, holidays, shoes, software, carpets, insurance, cars, mobile phones and a thousand other commodities.

When jewellery chain chief Gerald Ratner publicly described his products as 'crap' he was saying aloud what many chief executives have said to themselves privately and, indeed, a few have said in public.[4]

Once a company stops respecting its market, the chances are its corporate image will sooner or later start to reflect this contempt. It may come across as bullying tactics, or as a 'take it or leave it' attitude, or simply as a reduced level of service that will be interpreted by customers as 'we don't care about you any more'. However it materialises, that is the point at which customers stop being 'automatons' and start to exercise customer choice, usually by going to another supplier.

You can see this unconscious contempt today in the kind of assertions that many companies of all sizes make in their corporate statements. When a company says things like 'Our mission is total customer satisfaction', it is obvious that the company's thinking has gone off the rails. All commercial organisations are driven by a combination of commercial expediency and the desire for profit. Whatever a company's theoretical position may be, in practice the limits of its concern for others are the legal boundaries of consumer and safety law. In making this kind of phoney statement, the company's executives are really saying, 'we think you, our customers, our shareholders, our employees, so submissive and unsophisticated that you will accept anything we say as the truth'. The message may be analysed rationally only in books about company behaviour; but it will be interpreted instinctively that way by everyone.

Some large corporations have responded to the greater visibility of the 'see-through' society and to the rise of these new, powerful constituencies around them by becoming more relaxed, more open, and seeing mutual benefits in opening and maintaining channels of communication with those outside, especially customers and the press. Sadly, many more have reacted rather like the patriarch of a Victorian family who senses his authority being challenged by his teenage children.

This attempt by companies to reassert the authoritative position they once enjoyed expresses itself in many ways, one of which might perhaps be called the 'Coca-Cola syndrome'.

How Coca-Cola Changed the Taste of Coke

Coca-Cola's chief executive, Roberto Goizueta, and his fellow directors, received some welcome news at the company's Atlanta, Georgia, headquarters in the hot summer of 1991; news that put a smile back on their faces – and not before time.

Hot weather always brings a smile to the face of a soft drinks company. But the cause for celebration this time was a survey of 6,000 famous brands in eleven countries, which showed that Coca-Cola was the most powerful and successful brand name in the world. Even better was the news that Coke's bitter long-time rival Pepsi was down in tenth position – and even McDonald's could only manage eighth place.

The news came at the end of what, for the soft drinks firm, had been a tumultuous decade of ups and downs, during which it had come perilously close to throwing away its market leadership by a single irrational act.

When Roberto Goizueta became chairman and chief executive in 1981, he inherited one of the world's wealthiest and most powerful corporations. But the company was under increasing pressure from old and new rivals and the market was beginning to demand change. There had been signs of these new pressures – and intimations of deep flaws in Coke's corporate psyche – in the mid 1970s. But the warning signals had gone unrecognised or, more likely, were simply ignored.

The business that Goizueta took over was founded in Atlanta in 1886 by pharmacist John Pemberton. In the premises of the Pemberton Chemical Company, the young entrepreneur eagerly researched new medicines and tonics, seeking one that would make his fortune. Pemberton had a penchant for secrecy, always insisting on writing down his formulas and keeping them locked away in a safe – a habit that is the origin of the mystery that still surrounds the recipe for the drink that his book-keeper, Frank Robinson, christened Coca-Cola.[5]

Pemberton was a better chemist than businessman and died without realising the success of the formula in his safe, selling the company to Atlanta pharmacist Asa Candler. An astute businessman, Candler turned Pemberton's 'tonic' in twenty years into a business that his partners sold in 1919 for $25 million. The company's meteoric growth continued. If you had bought just 50 of the one-dollar shares Coca-Cola offered for sale in 1919, they would today be worth considerably more than $1 million.

The company that Pemberton and Candler founded is high on the list of America's largest corporations, with revenues in 2000 in excess of $20 billion. It directly employs 30,000 people, but because of its method of selling through franchises set up around the world, it indirectly employs more than 600,000 – about the same number as employed by the British Government. As well as Coke, the company today makes Diet Coke, Fanta, Sprite, Lilt, Tab, Minute Maid and Five Alive.

The first sign of the problems that were to unbalance the company emerged in the 1970s. Almost since its inception, Coke had been dogged by its smaller rival, Pepsi. Coke managed to remain well ahead in market share but the smaller company always seemed to be coming up with audacious and unexpected moves that somehow grabbed the headlines. In the early 1970s, Pepsi pulled off its most audacious coup to date.[6]

It started challenging people in the streets to take the 'Pepsi challenge': to taste Coke and Pepsi in a blind test and say which they preferred. Most people preferred Pepsi – a fact that Pepsi was able to make the central claim of a devastatingly effective series of advertisements. The result was a rapid increase in Pepsi's share of the American soft drink market from 6 per cent to 14 per cent.

Coca-Cola's initial response to the 'challenge' was to dismiss it as an advertising stunt. To the Coca-Cola management it was inconceivable that people really could like Pepsi more: Coke 'knew' that its product was best. Eisenhower had ordered it for the troops in World War Two; it was the official soft drink served at the White House; Coke had been drunk by astronauts on the Moon, for heaven's sake!

When Coca-Cola eventually got round to conducting market research by actually asking its customers which they preferred, it discovered that the Pepsi campaign wasn't all hype: people really did prefer the other product. By 1979, Pepsi had increased its share still further to 18 per cent, compared to Coke's 24 per cent. What was worrying to Coke was that it was spending $100 million more than Pepsi on advertising. Even worse, it had twice the number of vending machines and commanded twice the shelf space in supermarkets. This discovery shook Coca-Cola enough to set it questioning its own secret recipe and started it researching other formulae.

Once Roberto Goizueta took over in 1981, the company's research laboratory began responding to public demand for a low-calorie drink, and in 1982 it introduced the first fruits of its new research programme in the form of Diet Coke. This soon proved to be one of the most successful marketing stories of the early 1980s and one quickly emulated by all other soft drinks manufacturers. The company seemed back on course.

In the process of conducting the research that led to Diet Coke, the company tested many formulae other than the traditional Coke recipe on the panels of consumers it assembled. The traditional formula – the Pemberton formula – had been used for nearly a century and remained, officially, a closely-guarded company secret, although attempts to 'reverse engineer' the mysterious beverage suggest that it is the kind of drink made out of everyday ingredients in many drug stores in the last century. The main ingredients are water, sugar, caramel, phosphoric acid, caffeine and some natural flavourings, such as lemon.

Researchers looking for new and better drinks tested new Coke recipes on large numbers of consumer panels, both to get their reaction to the taste and their reaction to the idea of change. They asked questions like:

'If a new ingredient were added to Coke, would you be upset? Would you try the new drink?' The researchers estimated that about ten per cent of customers would be upset, and that half of these would get over it while the other half would not.[7]

However, this potential loss of five per cent was not as serious as it might seem, said Coca-Cola researchers, because those tested liked the new taste so much that the company estimated it would lead to gaining a one per cent increase in market share, worth $200 million annually.

The new flavour itself was sweeter – made with corn syrup instead of sugar – stickier and less fizzy: all the characteristics that the market said it wanted. People were no longer preferring Pepsi in a blind challenge: now it was new Coke they were choosing.

To make doubly sure it had got its research right, Coke invested a total of $4 million over two years in the biggest consumer taste test ever assembled. It asked 191,000 people in the 13 to 59 years age bracket to try a blind comparison of various Coke formulae and competitive products. Fifty-five per cent of those questioned chose the new Coke, beating not only old Coke but Pepsi as well.

This striking finding was the subject of many long board meetings in Atlanta. It seemed to bear out the results of the Pepsi challenge, and suggested that people didn't like existing Coke as much as the company thought they did. Any lingering doubts were silenced in 1984 when, despite the success of Diet Coke, for the first time in history, Coca-Cola's share of the soft drinks market fell almost two points, while Pepsi's market share continued to rise. Their competitor's growth was merely a fraction of a per cent but to the board of Coca-Cola it was like watching the seismograph registering the first distant tremor of an earthquake that could someday overwhelm them. Something had to be done.

Whether it was the statistics showing that a majority of people preferred the new formula, or whether it was simply the still painful and humiliating memory of the Pepsi challenge, the Coca-Cola board screwed up their courage to the sticking point and decided that they should go ahead and adopt the new formula. But one problem remained. Should they offer new Coke alongside the old? Or replace the Pemberton formula entirely?

This question was a tough one. Bottlers around the world would not take kindly to being told they would have to tool up to produce two brands instead of one. Equally, supermarkets would not wish to suddenly make twice the shelf space available simply to accommodate an additional Coke brand. Thus Coke took the fateful decision to abandon the Pemberton recipe and launch new improved Coke in its place.

The decision must have caused the PR department some misgivings, because they were about to prepare for the 100th anniversary of the Pemberton formula in only a year's time in 1986. But the die was cast: the McCann-Erickson advertising agency was briefed to introduce the American public to the new brand in an unprecedented multi-million dollar marketing campaign: by the end of the summer, the old Coke would disappear for good.

In April 1985, Roberto Goizueta announced to a major press conference in New York that Coke was to be replaced by a new brand. The news went down badly. Journalists left the meeting voicing skepticism and grumbling amongst themselves and the next morning many negative stories appeared.

The news also came as a bombshell to the bottlers and canning plants around the world. The bottling and labelling machines that had clanked night and day for decades, even during two world wars, were to fall silent. New cans and bottle labels were printed and delivered with the new concentrated cordial from which the drink was made. On the appointed day, the factories started to turn out new Coke.

The launch was accompanied by coast-to-coast hype. Millions of dollars were spent on magazine, poster and television advertising campaigns featuring Bill Cosby. New packs, new ring-pull cans, new bottles all proclaimed that Coke had changed and that a new era had begun. Because of the hype, millions of people rushed to experience the new taste and for a week or two sales rocketed as 150 million people tried the new Coke. Shipments to bottlers rose to the highest level for five years. The tension dissipated in the boardroom at Atlanta and bottles of the new drink were ceremonially opened as company executives and their wives toasted a successful launch.

After the hype had died down, it quickly became clear that a majority of Coke drinkers in the real world, as distinct from the world of consumer testing, didn't like the new formula – they found it too sweet and not fizzy enough. Within days, people were starting to complain to Coca-Cola's headquarters, to their local newspapers, and radio and TV stations. By mid-May, Atlanta was taking 5,000 calls of complaint a day, and angry letters by the sackful – the response was so great that the company had to take on new staff to cope. In total they received 40,000 letters of complaint.

In Seattle, loyalists who called themselves the Old Coke Drinkers of America made quixotic plans to file a class action lawsuit against Coca-Cola. Others, more pragmatic, began stockpiling the old Coke in their garages, and bottles started to change hands at black market prices.

One TV station commissioned a public opinion poll which found that, of those questioned, 59 per cent preferred the old Coke, 25 per cent preferred Pepsi and only 13 per cent liked the new Coke.

At first, the company reacted much as it had done at the Pepsi challenge. It was the customers who were wrong not the product. But the campaign against the new Coke became more and more vocal.

Coca-Cola commissioned its own research and discovered the awful truth. In early May, 53 per cent said they preferred the new brand. Within weeks this had dropped dramatically and by July only 30 per cent preferred new Coke.

Newspapers, radio and television began to feel that a national institution was under attack – like the Statue of Liberty or even the American flag. Robert Antonio, a University of Kansas sociologist, said that, 'some felt that a sacred symbol had been tampered with'. Roberto Goizueta's worst moment must have been when his own father spoke against the change to the press, jokingly threatening to disown his son. The word 'boycott' began to be heard in bars and factories.

Only four months after the launch, by July 1985, the company was facing a nationwide revolt against the new drink and had to back down. It announced a reversal of policy and promised that it would also continue to provide the old Pemberton flavour, now renamed 'Classic Coke' by the marketing wizards.

A new advertising campaign was hastily contrived, this time sending two different messages to Coke customers. Those who were happy with the change were invited to 'Catch the Wave' by a biker in sunglasses, while traditionalists were shown a conservative young man sitting on an old-fashioned jeep, with his faithful sheepdog, swigging thoughtfully from a can that promised, enigmatically, 'Red, White & You'.

What on earth had gone wrong? The company insisted it had based its decision on the finding that a sizeable majority of the test sample said they preferred the new formula. The difference between this majority and the minority who preferred the old taste in tests was indeed substantial – it was more than *twenty* times bigger than the sample needed to get a representative cross-section of the voters at a UK general election in order to predict the behaviour of 40 million British voters with fair accuracy.

But the lesson from Coke's experience is that even this large number was not at all representative when it came to predicting how Coke's hundreds of millions of customers would react when told their favourite drink was going to change. The researchers had asked people if they would try a new Coke; they had even asked them if they would be upset by a new Coke: but no one had told them that their traditional Coke was going to be taken away from them.

Had the market researchers asked people: would you like the new Coke to be the only Coke you can buy? the chances are they would have received a very different answer.

Whether it realised it or not, the company knew unconsciously that it had staked almost its entire future on the move it was planning, and everyone from the board to the shop floor knew that if things went wrong, the consequences could be disastrous. With this corporate anxiety hanging over them, the company unconsciously contrived its market studies to provide the answer it wanted to hear – like a mediaeval prince consulting his soothsayer. It was the wish for change prompted by fears of further loss of market share that came first: not the data that prompted it.

The problem was compounded because having made a huge marketing mistake, the company was reluctant to admit it and continued to insist that new Coke was better than the old – it was the customers

27

who were wrong. Coca-Cola got it wrong both ways: when it tried to change its customers' tastes and when it refused to listen to their protests. And for the same reason each time: the huge demand for its product had led it to delude itself into believing that it knew better than its own customers what they wanted. If it spent enough money on advertising, it could make the customers like whatever it chose to sell them.

And yet, as with the case of Shell, there is more to Coke's behaviour than merely corporate arrogance. The company had in effect made a major prophecy about its own future and made a total commitment to that prophecy. As we will see later, when prophecy fails, companies often emerge more convinced than ever of the rightness of their beliefs.

But if some companies see their customers merely as passive marketing units, easy to manipulate through the findings of depth psychology coupled with the persuading power of television advertising, how exactly do they see themselves in this equation?

CHAPTER THREE

MIRROR, MIRROR, ON THE WALL
How companies see themselves…and how McDonald's tried to silence its critics

The pale, severe, almond-shaped face is unmistakable. It stares defiantly from each of the dozen or so portraits of Queen Elizabeth I, Good Queen Bess, that remain in existence. Most striking of all, the paintings – whether in youth or old age, good or bad health, victory or defeat – are not merely similar, they are identical. The reason is that portrait artists of the time were issued with a cut-out template of the Queen's face together with a set of instructions on how she must be represented – or they were denied permission to reproduce the royal face at all.

There are plenty of chief executives today – of both sexes – who are as vain and manipulative as any mediaeval queen. But today's portraitists no longer take their orders from the Lord Chamberlain but from the readers of the daily newspapers. And those who seek to project a corporate image by queening it over the press and public are unlikely to succeed.

The method most often favoured by mediaeval monarchs to manage their 'corporate image' was that of censoring what people were allowed to see and to know, by managing the communication of information. Until the explosive growth of the Internet in recent years, little had changed in four centuries, and large corporations directed virtually their entire communications effort into managing what people could see and know.

One very damaging consequence of the monarchical approach to corporate image management is the tendency for the queen to start to believe she really is as beautiful as her portrait and for some companies to start to believe their own press releases – the Magic Mirror Syndrome.

This is a serious hazard for any large corporation – probably the greatest hazard from inside the company. Just as Snow White's wicked stepmother owned a magic mirror that she compelled daily to flatter her ego, so there is the danger that senior executives will try to force the corporate image to live up to their illusions.

Companies are like people in that they often change once they become successful. This change can take many forms, but one of the most hazardous from the point of view of how companies see themselves results in them becoming snobbish and remote. As a journalist, I see this phenomenon quite frequently. When I interview a chief executive I usually make a point of asking: 'Who exactly are your customers? What kind of people are they?'

Often, the ones who are going off the rails will pretend that their customer base consists exclusively of blue chip corporations, or the carriage trade, forgetting that when they were struggling in the recession a few years ago, they were grateful for customers like the fish and chip shop on the corner of the street, or people who had just cashed their unemployment cheque.

You might think this a harmless form of snobbery, like the spinster who puts out her best china when the vicar calls, but it is symptomatic of something rather more pathological. This form of snobbery is unhealthy because it breeds a sense of delusion that eventually infects how the company believes it is perceived. It is almost always mistaken – like the spinster who thinks the vicar secretly fancies her.

By contrast, some companies have a healthy, down-to-earth feel about them and an honest appreciation of their good points and bad points – an honesty you can sense at all levels when you go into their offices and meet people, in companies like Marks and Spencer, Hewlett-Packard and Safeway. Probably one reason for this openness is because to become a senior executive in these and similar companies, you have to get your hands dirty. In Safeway you have to stack the shelves and face up to the customer from hell – the demented parent with screaming children whose milk carton explodes ballistically on the check-out conveyor. On the other hand, it is possible to go a long way in Shell or BP simply by being an accountant or a petroleum geologist, without ever having sold so much as a litre of fuel or wiped a single windscreen. Even more remarkable, the chief executives of some supermarkets have never even shopped in their own stores, let alone worked in them.

Ultimately, it is this kind of lack of contact that leads some executives to lose their grip on their company's perception of itself without even realising they had it in their grasp in the first place.

Robert Townsend, in his 1970 account of Avis, *Up the Organisation*, gives a graphic picture of how every senior executive in Avis was obliged to spend a few weeks on the desk in airports and stations in the real world renting cars to busy customers. One such executive was joining Avis from academia, where he was an expert in corporate strategy and destined for high corporate office on the board. His two weeks on the desk was thought to be a mere formality. In fact, on his first morning at the desk when he was approached by a customer, he was so shocked at this unaccustomed human contact that he fainted.[1]

This kind of anecdote makes us smile: but I wonder how many more senior executives would faint if they were compelled to come face to face with the reality of their company and its effect on the world, rather than the cloud-cuckoo land that the boardroom culture of their companies induces them to inhabit?

The greatest danger of all in the Magic Mirror Syndrome is that the company's executives will use the corporation's powerful communications mechanisms as a smokescreen behind which they hide, so that they don't have to face critics in the press and among customers. Instead of being a friendly welcome to attract people in, the corporate image becomes a defensive moat to keep them out.

There is another common way in which senior executives can delude themselves; delusions that can express themselves as arrogant behaviour towards customers. When a company is highly successful, it is usually for one of a relatively small number of reasons: it has a monopoly or lack of serious competition (like British Telecom or Railtrack); there is an insatiable and insistent demand for its product or service (like Coca-Cola or British American Tobacco); raw material costs are minimal (like water utilities); or it has a highly-motivated sales force who are expert at

31

persuading customers into taking the product (like IBM in its heyday or double-glazing companies).

To some extent these matters can be managed. You can contrive to outperform your competitors by excelling on quality and service; you can contribute to creating a brisk demand through advertising and press relations. You can work hard to keep costs down. You can train and motivate an élite sales force. In the end, however, excellent management can have only a marginal effect on these factors. If the demand isn't there, if there are too many competitors, if costs are too high, if the customers won't be talked into buying, then the company is going to fail.

In the self-deluding company, however, senior executives congratulate themselves for all the wrong things. They start to believe that they are personally responsible for the demand for their products and services; that they are to be congratulated for their hard work and far-sightedness in having a near monopoly and that it is their brilliance as managers that has attracted such successful salespeople, or their cleverness as administrators that has produced such big profits.

Ironically, when the market turns against them – as it inevitably will one day – the same executives blame factors external to themselves and their companies: rising costs, changing fashion, 'the recession', duff sales staff – forgetting that a year before they were congratulating themselves on managing these very issues.

One way in which companies' self-delusion expresses itself publicly, and hence provides a direct clue to their unconscious self-perception, is in becoming obsessed with the need to come up with a memorable corporate slogan; one that cleverly sums up the company's business with a nifty *double entendre* that suggests all it ever thinks of are its customers and which projects a humane and caring image. A representative example of this genre is that of Ford Motor Company – 'Everything we do is driven by you'.

I believe that Ford and the many other exponents of such slogans are doing themselves a disservice with this kind of thing, because it contains the unconscious message 'we think we can win you over with clever words'. Every Ford customer (and everyone else in the world) knows that Ford does many things that are not driven by its customers. It lays off its cash reserves on the money market overnight; it makes people redundant when times are hard; it contributes to charities; it studies the Chancellor's statements anxiously for signs of changes that may adversely affect it; it makes millions of dollars in profits for its shareholders and executives. None of this is 'driven' by its customers, it is driven by commercial expediency and the desire for profit, just like every company the world over.

Probably an even worse objection to these clever phrases is not so much that they stick in people's throats but that in most cases it is impossible to say which companies they are talking about. Here is a list of some current corporate slogans of major organisations, taken from the pages of British national daily newspapers. How many companies can you identify? (The answers are given at the end of the book.) If you can identify even two or three, you are probably working in marketing or PR, or are employed by one of the companies. The overwhelming majority of people will be hard pressed to identify any of the slogans. Yet the companies they have been written for have collectively spent tens of millions of pounds advertising them nationally – money which most consumers will think could have been better spent improving product design or reducing prices.

The Communications Specialists
Lightening the Load
The art of performance
Let's make things better
Food for Thought
We're here to help
More than just a bank
Making life taste better
For ever for everyone
When all you want is everything
How switched on can you get?
Driven by passion
We care because you care
Whatever it takes
In Tune with People

Companies spend countless hours debating the hidden meanings of this or that slogan and millions of pounds in advertising them. Yet very few people are even able to remember which company they are associated with.

It seems to me that all these slogans highlight the fact that, to some extent, they are designed to conceal weaknesses in the companies that use them. Our real identity isn't good enough, they seem to be saying, let's puff ourselves up a bit. Benjamin Disraeli advised 'never complain and never explain'. There is a touch of both failings hanging nervously about these winsome phrases, creating an atmosphere of unconscious inferiority. By contrast there is something admirably bold and un-compromising about Virgin, Panasonic and Suzuki all of whom have (so far) avoided the slogan trap.

Looking over these slogans and the companies they belong to, I am also struck by a sense of confusion of identity, almost as though, when it came to thinking up a few words, the companies temporarily forgot who they really are.

Dixons, for instance, are not 'the communications experts'. They are experts at selling electronic goods in the high street. NatWest insist they are 'more than just a bank' but don't tell us what else it is they do – perhaps they too have become 'communications experts'?

Another danger of agonising over these weasel-word corporate slogans is that they may reinforce the sense of corporate self-delusion to the extent that directors actually begin to believe them and take their eye off the real ball-game.

In 2000, BP redesigned its corporate image and logo at a reported cost of £132 million, adopting the phrase 'Beyond petroleum'. It has also made and broadcast a series of TV advertisements designed to make people believe that the company is doing its bit in the fight against pollution of the atmosphere.

What is worrying is that the words the company has chosen to persuade us it is green (or rather that its advertising agency has chosen to persuade us) show exactly this kind of self-deluding approach.

In its ad, BP says, 'Can we drive our cars and still have cleaner air? We think so.'

The ads go on to tell us that 'BP is improving air quality in 50 major cities around the world and across the UK by introducing cleaner burning petrol and diesel fuel.'

The words used are undoubtedly true. But what the ad does not tell us is that around 25 per cent of atmospheric pollution is caused by car exhausts, so it is BP and its fellow oil companies who are partly responsible for polluting the air in the first place.

Moreover, the rate of pollution of the atmosphere by car exhausts is *growing*, not diminishing, for the simple reason that car usage is growing the world over. BP is selling more petrol every day, not less.[2]

What this means is that the central claims of BP's TV ads are simply not true. We cannot drive our cars and still have cleaner air. Driving cars does not make the air cleaner, it pollutes it further. The only way to stop polluting the air is to stop burning hydrocarbon fuels. And to say, as the company does, that it is 'improving air quality' is only true in the limited sense that BP's fuels are not polluting the atmosphere as much as they used to. It is, of course, very welcome to learn that modern fuels pollute less than the ones BP and others used to sell. But it is a very long way from that small blessing to the claims that BP is here making.

It is noticeable that some of the very large companies who have adopted a 'more money than sense' approach to corporate image manipulation in recent years seem to have recognised this danger, pulled themselves together and moved away from this kind of nonsense to simple and credible statements. A few years back, British Telecom saddled itself with the completely incredible 'It's you we answer to' (the one thing that almost every subscriber agrees BT does not do). It then adopted the more credible 'It's good to talk', and is now telling us to 'Stay in touch'. In dropping the pretence of being some kind of public benefactor and getting back to the business of making money, BT is both behaving honestly and getting back in touch with its real reason for being.

My personal favourite among this new breed of credible slogan, and the one I nominate for the Academy Award for Candour, is that of the sewage transport company whose bulk liquid lorries have on the side the slogan 'We Shovel Shit'. At least they know exactly who they are and what they do, and are not afraid to tell us.

The most important point here is that the things an organisation does and the things it says are a kind of sample of its wares. If its messages are slick, smoothly crafted, expensive words, then we, its customers, are likely to conclude that it will pay anything, do anything, say anything, no matter how insincere, to ingratiate itself with us. If its words are honest and straightforward, that is how the company will be seen.

Just what can happen when a giant corporation starts to believe its own press releases and becomes deaf to external criticism is well illustrated by the case of how McDonald's tried to silence its critics.

How McDonald's Tried to Silence its Critics

Of all the unpredictable courses of action that organisations sometimes embark on, the most risky by far is that of litigation. There is always the danger that even if the company wins the case, it will lose the corporate image battle. If the organisation is very big and the subject of litigation is unimportant, then perhaps this potential damage will not be a problem. But if the company allows the very core of its business to become the subject of litigation, it is playing Russian roulette with one of its most important assets.

Like many large corporations, the McDonald's hamburger chain has been the target of environmental and consumer groups over the years. McDonald's, however, is the most visible target in the high street. It is the world's biggest retail food outlet, with annual sales of more than $40 billion in 2000. It is also the world's biggest grower and user of beef. It is one of the biggest users of disposable packaging materials, and hence one of the biggest creators of waste.

In 1984, a small environmentalist group called London Greenpeace (it has no connection with Greenpeace International and seems to draw support mainly from vegetarians) began a campaign against McDonald's and published a leaflet called 'What's Wrong With McDonald's? – Everything They Don't Want You To Know.'[3]

On wet winter evenings, the protesters cut lonely figures as they stood on the cold pavements outside the brightly-lit restaurants, under the instantly-recognisable yellow McDonald's sign, handing leaflets to passers-by, most of whom were more interested in a Big Mac with French fries than in vegetarian protests.

The leaflets that ended up on the wet pavements made a number of specific allegations against McDonald's. That its promotion and sale of 'junk' food which is low in fibre but high in fat, saturated fat, salt and sugar content, was harmful because this kind of diet has been linked to heart disease and cancer. That McDonald's exploits children by its use of advertisements and gimmicks to sell unhealthy products. That the company destroys rain forests to provide grain feed for its cattle. That it 'tortures and murders' animals to supply meat. That its packaging is harmful to the environment. That McDonald's treats its staff badly and is hostile to unions.

The campaign gathered momentum through the late 1980s and the leaflet was distributed widely in Britain, America and elsewhere. McDonald's rejected the allegations and responded by employing private detectives and infiltrating them into London Greenpeace meetings. In September 1990, the company served writs for libel on five people connected with the group.[4]

Similar criticisms had been made by many environmentalists and consumerists in the United States, Britain and other European countries where McDonald's have fast food restaurants. However, only Britain has draconian libel laws that would enable the company to take such legal action. In the United States, for example, such a lawsuit would be unlikely because US law requires the company bringing the suit to prove that what was said was false, whereas in Britain, the defendants have to show that what they said is true.

Usually, when a large powerful corporation sues ordinary private individuals for libel, the individuals have no alternative but to settle out of court by agreeing to apologise publicly, retract their statements and pay whatever sum they can afford by way of damages – or face the possibility of complete financial ruin simply by defending themselves, even if they win.

In this case, McDonald's strategy initially seemed to be working. Told that there was no legal aid available to fight libel actions and that they stood little chance of even getting to trial, three of the five apologised to McDonald's. Then, things started to go wrong for the burger chain. The other two defendants, Helen Steel and Dave Morris, were unemployed with no personal assets to speak of and no resources to hire expensive lawyers. But they did have the moral support and advice of their fellow environmentalists. They had nothing to lose and a platform on which to publicise their complaints.

Refusing to be intimidated by McDonald's corporate might, Steel and Morris – quickly dubbed the 'McLibel Two' – declined to apologise and settle out of court, and instead began defending themselves in court in a case that McDonald's imagined would last 'three or four weeks' but which dragged on for two years, becoming the longest libel case in history and also dragging McDonald's through a PR nightmare by giving the allegations prolonged exposure.

McDonald's themselves were far more successful in spreading the allegations than the defendants could ever have been. Having given the views of their critics international prominence by suing them, McDonald's next printed and distributed a leaflet called 'Why McDonald's is Going to Court', which it made available nationally in all its restaurants, thus drawing further attention to the affair. In it, McDonald's said the London Greenpeace leaflet 'contains many statements about McDonald's which are not true and highly damaging'. It also said that the group had ignored requests to stop publishing the leaflet.[5]

When the trial came to court in June 1994, the two defendants were denied a jury trial at the request of McDonald's, who argued that the case was 'too complex' for a jury and it was thus heard by a judge sitting alone. Steel and Morris were also denied legal aid and were obliged to conduct their own defence.

The case was heard in the awe-inspiring marble halls of London's Royal Courts of Justice, where Steel and Morris were conspicuous figures among the wigs and gowns of the legal profession. Perhaps McDonald's and their advisers expected the two defendants to be over-awed by the circumstances and the gravity of the charges against them. If so, they were quickly disappointed for, with no resources and no legal training, the defendants mercilessly set about cross-examining all of McDonald's senior executives and expert witnesses on the stand over subsequent months and compelled them to admit that, in essence, many of the criticisms contained in the leaflet are true.

When he opened the prosecution, McDonald's chief legal counsel, Richard Rampton QC, told the court that London Greenpeace's claims about the company's hamburgers being linked to heart disease and cancer was the most central and defamatory allegation. If this allegation were proven, he said, it would be the 'kiss of death' for a fast food company like McDonald's. These words came back to haunt the prosecution over the coming months as Steel and Morris' evidence and cross-examination showed the allegation to be supported by leading medical opinion.[6]

One of the first expert witnesses to take the stand on McDonald's behalf was an expert on cancer, Dr Sydney Arnott. Steel and Morris asked his opinion of the statement that 'A diet high in fat, sugar, animal products and salt and low in fibre, vitamins and minerals is linked with cancer of the breast and bowel and heart disease.' Dr Arnott replied that 'If it is being directed to the public then I would say it is a very reasonable thing to say.' The defendants then explained that the statement was taken from the leaflet that McDonald's claimed was libellous.[7]

McDonald's next expert witness, Professor Verner Wheelock, fared no better. He admitted that there is a considerable amount of evidence that diseases such as obesity, diabetes, high blood pressure, heart disease, stroke and some forms of cancer are related to a diet high in fat, saturated fat, salt and sugar, and low in dietary fibre. He also admitted that a typical McDonald's meal was high in fat, saturated fat and salt content and would not come within dietary recommendations. He accepted, too, that people were attracted to high levels of sugar and salt and found it hard to give up the taste.[8]

A stream of expert witnesses for the defence testified that McDonald's food was unhealthy. Dr Neal Barnard, president of the US Physicians' Committee for Responsible Medicine, and an expert on nutrition, said that 'Many products sold by McDonald's are high in fat and cholesterol, and low in fibre and certain vitamins,' and that the products, 'contribute to heart disease, certain forms of cancer and other diseases'. He said that the links between diet and these diseases were 'established beyond any reasonable doubt' and were causal links. [9]

Dr Barnard also said that 'McDonald's food remains part of the problem, rather than part of the solution' and he quoted the director of a study into heart disease, Dr William Castelli, who said: 'When you see the Golden Arches you're probably on the road to the Pearly Gates.'

As the trial progressed, so much evidence was presented as to the unhealthiness of McDonald's food that the burger chain's counsel, Richard Rampton, intervened to say that his client was not objecting to the description of their food as 'junk food'.

After the presentation of much blood-curdling evidence as to the conditions in which McDonald's raised and slaughtered the cattle and chickens to make its hamburgers, McDonald's counsel intervened again to announce that his client were no longer objecting to the terms 'torture' and 'murder' being used to describe the rearing and slaughter of its animals. [10]

Probably the worst moment of the trial from McDonald's corporate image point of view was when the defendants read into the record a statement by the actor who used to play the clown Ronald McDonald saying, 'I brainwashed youngsters into doing wrong. I want to say sorry to children everywhere for selling out to concerns who make millions by murdering animals.' [11]

As this drama degenerated into a cross between Greek tragedy and French farce, the press began to take an interest and to report the case. Regular updates appeared on the Internet in newsgroups such as alt.censorship, and websites such as www.mcspotlight.org.

As time went on, it became clear that there was a real possibility the court might find for the defendants, and soon the positions of the plaintiff and defendants were reversed, with senior McDonald's executives flying over the Atlantic to attempt to make a deal with Steel and Morris to get them to settle out of court.

According to Mike Love, a former Conservative Party strategist hired by McDonald's to run its UK public relations, the company was 'not seeking a way out of the case'. Love said: 'We're confident of the strength of our case and we're seeking a judgement at the end of the case.'

He added that 'discussions have taken place [with Steel and Morris] and I think you would expect that to happen in a trial of this length. We only reluctantly came to court after 10 years.'

According to Steel and Morris however, 'McDonald's at their own initiative have twice called discussions with [us] in order to pursue ways of ending the case. At both meetings members of the US Board of Directors have flown into London at 24hrs notice to meet with us...

'Our position today is clear. Our pre-conditions for allowing the McDonald's Corporation to withdraw from the case are:

1) We call on McDonald's to give an undertaking not to sue any organisation or individuals for making statements similar to those contained in the London Greenpeace Factsheet.

2) We call on McDonald's to apologise to those people they have sued in the past for such statements.

3) We call on McDonald's to pay a substantial sum to a mutually agreeable third party in lieu of compensation to us.' [12]

As with the case of Intel (see Chapter Five) the McDonald's story was first made public through the Internet, and it was primarily through this source that the story was later picked up by national newspapers such as the *Guardian*, the *Independent* and *Wall Street Journal*. This is a significant change in reporting practice for, in the past, many newspapers would not touch a libel case in progress for fear that the court might find against the defendant and the newspapers themselves would thus also be vulnerable to litigation for damages for having repeated the libel.

In this case, sections of the press were outraged at McDonald's behaviour. The *Independent*, for example, printed a leader which said, in part, 'There is a long and lively tradition in this country of robust comment by individuals and pressure groups about the powerful and wealthy; so the use of the libel laws to prevent leaflets being handed out seems oppressive.

'Although the burger giant chose to confront the problem with writs, it could have decided to do it by argument. The resources McDonald's has available for public relations and promotions dwarfs the total budget of many a small nation. So would it have been beyond it to enter a public debate in which it met its critics and answered them on every point? Could it not have handed out leaflets of its own, or devoted some of its TV ad time to dealing with these issues?

'The trouble is that this is not how some companies see their relationship with us; we are passive consumers of product and image. A discussion about diet, waste or employment practice might just detract from the rosy, uncomplicated message they want us to absorb.'

The *Independent* leader concluded, 'As the Shell saga showed, it is now impossible to treat campaigners as though they are criminal lunatics and public opinion as something to be bought through parliamentary lobbying. There is an increasing public demand that large and powerful companies should take our sensibilities into account when making decisions or framing strategies. McDonald's should recognise this, drop its libel action and begin the debate.'

On 19 June 1997, the judge delivered his findings. He said that Steel and Morris had not proved their allegations against McDonald's on rain forest destruction, packaging, food poisoning, starvation in the third world, heart disease and cancer, and bad working conditions. But he found the defendants had proved that McDonald's 'exploit children' with their advertising, falsely advertise their food as nutritious, risk the health of their long-term regular customers, are 'culpably responsible' for cruelty to animals reared for their products, are 'strongly antipathetic' to unions, and pay their workers low wages.[13]

The judge ruled that Steel and Morris had libelled McDonald's but, as they had proved many of their allegations, the burger firm would only be awarded half their claimed damages.

Steel and Morris have appealed to the House of Lords and are now campaigning for changes to the libel laws. Whatever the outcome, it seems unlikely that any large corporation will be so foolish as to resort to this kind of litigation again.

It is when they fall victim to the Magic Mirror Syndrome and begin to believe their own press releases that companies conceive a desire to portray themselves and their products in a 'rosy and uncomplicated' way that they expect us to absorb unquestioningly. Yet it is at precisely this stage that many companies are at their most self-deluding, as the next examples show.

CHAPTER FOUR

LITTLE WHITE LIES
How companies portray themselves...*and how Kenco flavoured its TV ads*

One of the many paradoxes of the corporate mind is that, although large companies are often sensitive and even paranoid about how they are perceived, they are also remarkably careless of safeguarding their corporate image.

Every business school in the world drums into its MBA students one golden rule: when you are running the show, whatever you do, don't bet the company. Most companies are set up so that it is virtually impossible for a single individual to imperil the entire organisation by his or her actions. One notable exception to this rule was Barings Bank, where a single futures trader, Nick Leeson, sitting at a computer screen in Singapore, was able to gamble away the firm's entire cash holdings playing the Far Eastern market while his colleagues in London slept. Most companies view such an incident with horror and amazement: 'It could never happen to us.'

Yet in many of the world's corporations it remains possible for one or a few individuals to risk the corporate image on hare-brained gambles, and this game of corporate Russian roulette is regarded with something like indifference by many of their fellow executives.

In some organisations, an issue like the corporate image is regarded as being of such minor importance in comparison with the real macho stuff, like sales and finance and production and industrial relations, that it is delegated to the marketing director to handle alone – or even a junior executive. If he or she lacks the necessary gravitas or experience, the

44

marketing director will call on outside marketing consultants or advertising agents.

By this unplanned, roundabout but often trodden route, one of the corporation's most valuable assets can fall into the hands of relatively young, inexperienced outsiders who know little or nothing of the organisation and owe it nothing beyond a day's work for the day's pay they will receive for the advice they tender.

Some advertising agencies have come to exert a powerful influence over their clients as far as their corporate image is concerned. Most agencies today offer the entire spectrum of marketing consultancy services, quite apart from the business of designing, writing and placing ads. Because large agencies provide such a wide spectrum of professional services that are essential to building and maintaining a corporate image, the keys to the corporate image often end up being held by the agency. In some cases this is a little like the keys to the Tower of London being held by the milkman: both the amount of authority and the importance of the task are almost certainly too great to be invested in an outside supplier, however skilful.

Another peculiarity of corporate image management is that different managers, depending on their role in the organisation, perceive the subject itself in different ways. To some managers, rebuilding the corporate image simply means employing a graphic designer to do a re-badging job. Those managers who have thought the process through in more depth know that the organisation's important stakeholders are affected by much more than simply logos and letterheads. They are affected by the things the company says; by the things it does; by the products and services it markets; by the actions and attitudes of the individuals who work for the organisation. The corporate image is not merely a matter of superficial gloss: it involves the very heart of the organisation.

The level of some companies' awareness about their effect on their customers and prospective customers is so low as to be astounding. Take, for example, the case of companies that depend to a very high degree on direct mail for their sales, companies like Reader's Digest, or Littlewoods Mail Order.

The response that companies such as this receive to their mailing campaigns is very low, as low as one per cent – the remainder of each costly mailing goes straight into the waste-basket. At the same time, the scale of some of the mailings can be very high – in some extraordinary cases even involving millions of homes.

No one in these organisations seems to be concerned that they have created a marketing tool that necessarily involves causing hundreds of thousands of prospective customers to take an expensive example of the company's name, its corporate livery and its products, and throw them straight into the bin, quite possibly accompanied by feelings of irritation and disdain for the company and its products. Nor that, having compelled 99 per cent of their own market to perform this act of symbolic rejection, reinforcing their negative feelings about a company that deliberately originates such trash, they compel them to do it all over again the following month. The personal equivalent would be sending out a photograph of oneself and inviting the recipients to use it as a dartboard.

TV comedian Jack Dee, famed for his acid view of life, once told his audience, 'I'm so unlucky; I'm the only man in Britain who received a letter from Reader's Digest telling me that my name has *not* been selected for their prize draw.' When television comedians start telling jokes about your company and your product, it's time to start worrying, as Intel was to discover.

All of the things the company does and all of the things it says draw from a single well; what one might loosely call the company's 'story'. The company story is a complex, dynamic, organic creation that is part myth, part wishful thinking, part hard fact, part history, part future plan. This strange hybrid informs everything that communicates who and what the company is to the world. It is the company story that differentiates each organisation from any other group of people who have come together to co-operate in the business of making money.

The company story is one area where the transformation of the press into a serious interest group can have an important effect on how the company portrays itself: if it strays from the straight and narrow truth at all in its corporate story – even with little white lies – it is far more likely today to be found out and publicly condemned.

The effect of this can be out of all proportion to the offence if the company has relied on untruths in any way. For example, Anita Roddick's Body Shop built up a reputation for its caring attitude to the third world. Later it was widely pilloried in the press for hypocrisy and accused of exploiting third world workers, with the result that sales were affected. The company should have been winning Brownie points for being green but instead received a punishing dent in its halo for having tried to be seen as holier than the rest of us.

There was a time when even the reptiles of the tabloid press considered it unsporting to comment on lapses of taste or 'errors of fact' by the great and the good as when, in a more innocent age, the British press closed ranks and kept uniformly quiet about the affair between King Edward and Wallis Simpson. Today, of course, the media feels no such compunction about publishing even the seediest details of the highest in the land, including the grass stains on the knees of the royal pyjamas.

Strangely, even when the perceived taboo against printing stories about the powerful had evaporated from the British Royal Family, an aura of inviolability somehow lingered around major British corporations, as though it would be unpatriotic and un-British to attack such institutions as Shell or British Airways or BT. As recently as the late 1970s and early 1980s such corporations tended to be handled with kid gloves by the press. Even as recently as the 1990s no publication, with the sole exception of the satirical magazine *Private Eye*, dared to say of Robert Maxwell, chairman of Mirror Group Newspapers, what is obvious with hindsight – that he was an unscrupulous crook who should never have been trusted with other people's money.

Even the most trivial deceit can come back to haunt a company. The Kenco coffee company built a whole series of television advertisements around the idea that Kenco itself has acquired a new woman chief executive, who has acted like a new broom and swept away the old fuddy-duddy ideas of the previously male-dominated board. The problem with the campaign emerged when the *Daily Mail* got onto the fact that Kenco does not have a new woman chief executive, that the whole thing is a fiction, and that the company has in fact just the kind of traditional male-dominated board that its advertisements ridicule.

Some executives might respond to cases such as these by saying, 'So what? It's only an advertisement.' The trouble is that, whether companies realise it or not, the advertisement is the means by which the corporation communicates unconsciously to its customers what it is *really like*. If a company tells lies in its ads, it is playing with fire.

To avoid even the appearance of behaving deceitfully, companies need to go through their story, and their practices, in relation to all the sensitive environmental and consumer issues, very carefully to get rid of or stop anything that is suspect. It doesn't matter how ethical the company *says* it is, and it doesn't matter how many good things it does – if there is an ugly blot somewhere, it will be discovered.

There are two specific areas where companies need to take the growing influence of environmentalist and consumerist groups into their calculations. The first is in ensuring consistency in their policies and the second is in ensuring that they are not shooting themselves in the foot.

It was lack of consistency that let Shell down over the Brent Spar affair. As mentioned earlier, the company has been very active in supporting environmental issues for decades. There can be little doubt that those managers within the company responsible for environmental issues must be spitting feathers over the way their policies were jettisoned in the name of expediency. These people had a major contribution to make to Shell's overall corporate strategy but were ignored. But this, of course, is the heart of the problem and the very issue that should have been addressed. It is not just the damage which Brent Spar would have done to the environment that matters: it is the damage it has done to our perception of Shell.

The second issue is simply that of avoiding careless moves that are eminently avoidable. Some advertising agencies, for example, have perceived environmental issues as an opportunity for a little creative copywriting to make their clients appear 'green'.

Environmentalists such as Friends of the Earth keep a sharp eye open for this sort of thing and, when they spot them, are only too happy to alert the press.[1]

For instance, Higgs Furs advertised its fox furs as being 'environmentally friendly' on the grounds that they contained only natural products and nothing synthetic – an entirely new meaning for the word 'friendly'.[2]

Fisons advertised its peat-based compost saying that it 'in no way endangers our remaining wetlands' when in fact 90 per cent of Fisons' peat cutting was on peat bogs designated as areas of Special Scientific Interest.[3]

Eastern Electricity urged homeowners to 'use more electricity rather than less', as a means to combat global warming on the grounds that 'there is very little CO_2 or global warming gas emissions from the all electrical home'. Eastern chose to ignore the fact that emissions from the power stations supplying those homes are the UK's *biggest* contributors to global warming.[4]

This sort of thing may well have elicited gales of cynical laughter in the boardroom when the idea was floated by the agency. But it was also inevitable that the companies would be found out and shopped to the press by environmentalists. The downside is not so much the ephemeral flurry of bad publicity, as the lasting impression left in our minds that the organisations concerned cynically see environmental issues as a trivial nuisance that are merely an obstacle to making money.

The Advertising Standards Authority has already published a report condemning this kind of thing. According to the ASA, 'Some advertisers seem to be paying more attention to making sure their wares are perceived as sitting on the right side of the green fence than to checking the factual accuracy of their claims...advertisers have a special duty to ensure accuracy in an area where even the scientists are not absolutely sure of their facts.'[5]

How Kenco Flavoured its TV Ads

Television advertising is fertile ground for the corporate mind. Through the miracle of Hollywood-type special effects and digital image processing, the wildest dreams and self-delusions of companies of all kinds unfold nightly on the screens in our living rooms.

Environmentally-conscious motor car manufacturers make beautiful wild flowers spring from the hedgerows as their vehicles whizz sensitively past; soap powders miraculously produce dazzling whiteness in vests that even *Die Hard* star Bruce Willis would be ashamed to put in the laundry basket; milk bottles dance joyously up the garden path at the milkman's command; chimpanzees enjoy a refreshing cup of tea around their living-room fire.

One especially interesting advertising phenomenon was the long-running series of ads on behalf of the instant coffee produced by the Kenco Coffee Company. The advertisements tell a story which begins with the arrival of a determined young woman in the boardroom of the Kenco company itself. Her presence causes something of a stir among the board, who are uniformly male, getting on in years and obviously very set in their ways. [6]

The new face in the boardroom is played by talented actress Cheri Lunghi, who had previously starred in a successful TV series called 'The Manager'. In this series, Miss Lunghi dramatically portrayed a woman succeeding against the odds in a man's world as the manager of a professional football team.

In the Kenco coffee ads, we quickly learn that the character played by Miss Lunghi is a woman succeeding against the odds in a man's world. She plays the daughter of Kenco's former boss and has taken over the reins, determined to be a new broom in the stuffy corridors of male power. She coolly informs the assembled board members that she has decided Kenco will enter the brash new world of instant coffee – a far cry from the conservative traditions of the ground coffee business, with its old-world processes of roasting and grinding beans and its snobbish distinctions of Jamaica Blue Mountain versus Costa Rican beans.

The new managing director's plans send a frisson of alarm through the old boys around the table, as they sip their coffee from the traditional bone china cups. How, they demand to know from this upstart woman, can she ever hope to make an instant coffee that could compete with the incomparable flavour of Kenco traditional ground coffee?

The confident young woman merely smiles as one by one the old boys realise that without noticing, they have been drinking the new instant coffee, and unknowingly giving it their tacit approval.

Later advertisements in the series depict further excursions by the young woman into the man's world of coffee growing, bringing about sweeping changes. We see her visiting plantations in exotic foreign locations in South America and the Caribbean; we see her being mistaken for a lowly female assistant before putting the local growers in their place by buying their entire crop of top quality beans. In one advertisement an ageing plantation owner tactlessly sympathises with her: 'It must have been a blow to the old man not to have a son to carry on the business.' Like all the other male chauvinists, he too is caught out by the instant coffee that tastes, we are told, just like old-fashioned ground coffee.

At one level, it's easy to appreciate the skill and careful thought with which this series of advertisements has been constructed. They are clearly aimed at women buyers (the majority of supermarket shoppers still being women) and equally aimed at breaking down prejudices against instant coffee among older consumers. They appear to achieve these aims very effectively.

As a writer, I admire the talent and technical skill with which the ads have been developed in response to careful market research and analysis of buying habits.

Yet at another level, the ads give, I believe, cause for concern. Everyone recognises that we are here in the cloud-cuckoo-land of advertising and not in the real world. No one watching will confuse the actors and actresses with real people. Everyone knows that considerable license is permissible in dramatising the attractiveness of this or that product. But the Kenco ad broke new ground in a specific and worrying way in that it deliberately made up a little play about something that could be true, and would add to the credit of the company if it were true, but that in fact isn't true at all.

Most advertisements exaggerate or distort in some way or another, and these distortions are not normally cause for serious complaint. In another recent advertisement, Olympic athlete Carl Lewis was seen apparently running across the Atlantic Ocean and up the Statue of Liberty in New

York, to advertise Pirelli tyres. No one imagines that Lewis actually can run on water or that he really climbs the famous statue.

But the Kenco ad is subtly different. Kenco was founded by a real businessman, no doubt an astute one; someone who knew all there is to know about importing coffee and supplying a roast and blend that has satisfied millions of customers. He was very likely a bit of a perfectionist and demanded much from his staff. It is easy to imagine that he would have liked to have someone to carry on his business after him: easy to imagine an enterprising daughter who was a chip off the old block and who was just as tough and shrewd a boss as the old man. It is possible to imagine all this, as the advertising agency has done so skilfully, but that is all it is – imaginary.

Of course, it would be absurd to be shocked by this deception, which is trivial in comparison with the routine dissemination of lies, half-truths and distortions by practically every large organisation in the world, including the government. But what I think does give pause for thought is the deliberate nature of the deception.

No one in their right mind could imagine that Carl Lewis can run across the Atlantic: but almost everyone, unless they have been given the true facts, is likely to believe the substance of the Kenco advertisement. And, what is more, that is precisely the intention of the company and its advertising agency: to blur the line between fact and fiction; to deceive us as to the facts to put themselves in a better light in order to make money out of us.

The body that investigates complaints about advertisements broadcast on TV in Britain is the Independent Television Commission. The ITC says it received only three complaints about the advertisement, criticising it for being misleading. Kenco itself defended the advertisements, saying that using an actress to portray a new female boss was 'a visual metaphor indicating that the company has a contemporary outlook'.[7]

The ITC did not uphold the complaints because, it said, the advertisement was not materially misleading as to the *product itself*, and thus the complaints were about a matter outside its power to adjudicate.

The problem with this kind of thing, it seems to me, is that it raises questions about the advertiser's trustworthiness. Kenco says that its coffee is made from the very highest quality beans. But if it is willing to tell little white lies about its management and its policy on women executives, how are we to know whether it is also willing to tell little white lies about its coffee? Maybe it doesn't use the very highest quality beans but only the next best quality, which most of us could not tell apart? Maybe it even chucks in a few old wrestlers' jock straps and rugby players' underpants to the mix when no one is looking? It seems to me that the company has only itself to blame if we, the buyers, are no longer able to tell how far Kenco is willing to go in distorting the facts for commercial gain.

The Kenco ads, and others like them, serve to make us realise that some large, powerful, wealthy corporations do not feel honour bound to tell the strict truth to us, their customers. Some feel that little white lies are permissible. Yet strangely, at the same time, the directors of *all* companies, including Kenco and everyone else who advertises, would be outraged to hear such a suggestion and, on the contrary, would pride themselves on their integrity and truthfulness.

This paradox illustrates that the kind of lying indulged in by some advertisers is entirely unconscious. They are not even aware that they are doing anything reprehensible because they have shut away that knowledge from their conscious perception of themselves and the way they do business.

From the point of view of us, the consumers, this finding sadly means only one thing: it is safer to distrust *everything* that a corporation tells you, unless it can prove that what it is saying is true. Increasingly, companies in future are going to have to prove their words.

CHAPTER FIVE

JUST A TINY MISTAKE

How companies see their critics...*and how Intel got its sums wrong*

There is very much less than meets the eye to most large or important organisations. Outwardly, *The Times'* top 1000 companies, and Britain's most prestigious or important public institutions and organisations present a monolithic façade, apparently impenetrable at any level, and coolly impervious to outside influence or criticism.

In reality, this image of the rhinoceros-like organisation hardly even noticing the pin-pricks of corporate critics, is part of the public relations front. The truth is that almost all large and important organisations are excessively sensitive to the slightest criticism, and are highly vulnerable to the actions of even a single determined outsider.

When the most notorious British espionage traitor of all time, Kim Philby, succeeded with remarkable ease in penetrating the inner sanctum of the British establishment, the Secret Intelligence Service, his KGB controller thought he had merely penetrated a cover organisation rather than the real secret service. The organisation Philby described in his reports was not the legendary SIS but one poorly organised and staffed, ignorant in its intelligence gathering, and banal in its operations – doing little more than clipping newspaper cuttings and putting them into cardboard files marked 'Top Secret'. Tragically, it was no cleverly conceived cover plan: Philby had been admitted to the real thing. [1]

When legendary FBI chief J Edgar Hoover died and his much feared secret files were finally opened, they too were found to contain little more than newspaper clippings and banal reports of neighbours' gossip and suspicions. The chief's omnipotence had also been just an illusion, like the Wizard of Oz's magnifying mirror and voice amplifier.[2]

Perhaps the most persistent aspect of the myth of the monolithic organisation is the idea that, behind its closed boardroom doors, the chief executive and his or her senior colleagues are conspiring together to achieve some secret aim that is inimical to the public interest or to the organisation's critics.

The reality is that most people who work inside large organisations do not even know what each other's jobs are. The few senior people who do know are generally too suspicious of their colleagues ever to enter into any conspiracy with them. The corporate executive game consists in trying to gain some advance up the corporate ladder without sliding back down a corporate snake – being found out in any kind of conspiracy is a guaranteed ticket back to square one. The hallmark of most large organisations is not conspiracy but rather collective incompetence bred of mutual suspicion.

Instead, the origin of the myth of corporate invulnerability lies in the corporate unconscious – in wishful thinking on the part of its senior staff. A major factor in motivating some people to join a large, hierarchical organisation is the desire for the feeling of security that comes from being one of a large family group: the feeling of safety in numbers.

Having gained this strongly desired feeling of security by obtaining a coveted place on the inside, many corporate employees then mentally pull up the drawbridge: they act to confirm and reinforce their perceived privileged place at every opportunity. One of the simplest and most direct forms that this confirmation takes is to pretend that those inside the castle are invulnerable by ignoring or denigrating people who are on the outside.

When companies really do try to conspire, by trying to concert some strategy to silence their critics, or get the edge on their competitors, the results are usually the worst kind of bungled pantomime: as when McDonald's sued London Greenpeace or British Airways targeted Virgin Airways.

Just how vulnerable the imposing castle walls of large organisations can be to a single well-aimed shot is shown by the case of Intel Corporation and the chip that didn't add up.

How Intel Got its Sums Wrong

More than 100 million people around the world have Intel's product on their desks and in their homes, but until recently most people had never heard of Intel Corporation.

Twenty-five years ago, Intel became the first of the innovative firms in California's silicon valley to put an entire computer central processor on a single chip, the chip that is the heart of the desktop Personal Computer. The company has its imitators and it licenses some other chip makers to manufacture its designs, but it has consistently kept hold of more than 80 per cent of the world market for computer chips by a programme of continuous technical innovation. It produced the first 8-bit chip (the original Personal Computer), the first 16-bit chip (the 286 PC), the first 32-bit chip (386 and 486 machines) and the first 64-bit chip (the Pentium processor).[3]

However, although it has successfully dominated the computer chip market through successive invention, Intel suffered from a major disadvantage from a corporate recognition standpoint – that its product is always invisible to the end user, buried inside a box with someone else's badge on the outside. Thus it was Compaq, Dell or IBM who got the brand-name recognition.

In 1989, Intel decided to do something to make itself more visible and embarked on a programme of television, newspaper and magazine advertising promoting its 'Intel Inside' campaign, at a cost of many millions. The campaign was immensely successful and achieved the effect of giving Intel very high visibility. Unfortunately, at just the same moment that the firm's marketing department was scoring a world-wide success in increased corporate recognition, the product design department scored an equally dramatic own-goal.

In May 1994, Intel engineers going through the design of the Pentium chip with a fine tooth-comb discovered that they had made a minute mistake. At Intel's Palo Alto headquarters, a flurry of urgent email memos began to pile up on people's desktops and worried faces appeared in the elevators as the corporate pulse quickened. Lights burned in the windows late into the night. Thousands of customers had bought Pentium machines: millions more were expected to. The problem could be serious. It was like finding a fault in the first Model T Fords coming off the production line.

The design team ran checks on computers using the Pentium and quite quickly the corporate pulse returned to normal. The investigators came to the conclusion that the error was not significant because it would only crop up, they said, once every nine billion calculations. For the average spreadsheet user, this would cause an error (or what Intel's PR department would later coyly prefer to call 'a lack of precision') once every 27,000 years and so could safely be ignored, they thought. The company decided not to announce its discovery but to carry on with the world-wide product roll-out.

Nemesis, however, was waiting in the wings in the unlikely form of Dr Thomas Nicely, a professor of mathematics. In October 1994, Dr Nicely was running calculations on a brand new Pentium processor in his laboratory as part of his research and discovered the flaw that had kept the Intel engineers up all night six months earlier. It showed up as an error in the ninth decimal place of one of his calculations. Dr Nicely sat down at the keyboard of his PC and posted a message on the Internet noting his discovery.[4]

This innocent announcement quickly snowballed and, over the next few weeks, the issue became a hot topic on the Internet. People who had bought Pentium machines felt angry and betrayed that Intel knew about the problem and had apparently done nothing. According to Intel's Jim Jarrett, head of the company's investor relations, 'Based on the analytical work we had done on the problem we felt that replacement was unnecessary. We acknowledged that a few users like Dr Nicely were doing work that combined amounts of massive floating point calculations and the need for extreme precision and we said we would replace the processor for these people.'

As the national media got hold of the story from the Internet, things worsened. The flurry of activity at Intel's headquarters earlier in the year was now dwarfed as the company started a major damage limitation exercise. A task force of engineers, marketing people and senior executives was formed to concert strategy and deal with complaints. This task force quickly grew in size to 25 staff. Other Intel employees started volunteering to answer the freephone helplines as thousands of calls poured in from angry and confused customers who had heard about the problem and were naturally concerned. How serious was the fault? Would they be getting a free replacement chip? Why were only scientific big-wigs being given this special treatment?

By the end of November, a month after Dr Nicely had alerted the Internet to the flaw, it had become obvious that Intel had to take some more concrete action. The internal task force was by now being headed personally by Intel's chief executive, Andy Groves, and the team met to decide their next move. Yet still, despite the rising tide of resentment among customers, they decided against simply offering to replace every Pentium processor on the grounds that it would be too expensive, that it wasn't necessary, and that it would set a dangerous precedent for the future.

Instead, Andy Groves decided to issue a personal statement to users at the end of November 1994. Interestingly, the medium he chose for this message was the Internet – the instrument by which Intel's problem had first been exposed, and probably the first time in history that a chief executive had attempted to deal with a major consumer issue over the information superhighway.[5]

Groves' message was intended to calm customers' fears and defuse the situation, but it failed to do the trick. If anything, it made matters worse. In his message, Groves said: 'We will stand behind these chips for the life of your computer.' But the message said nothing about guaranteeing to exchange faulty chips for good ones. Instead, the message spoke vaguely about 'finding all users of Pentium chips engaged in heavy-duty calculations' and ended with a classic piece of corporate evasion: 'We remain dedicated to bringing [the Pentium processor] as close to perfection as possible.'[6]

It was this kind of stuff that made some Internet users suspect that the letter was not even from Andy Groves but was merely a bromide concocted by the PR department.

Despite the ground swell of discontent, Intel might just have weathered the storm had it not been for the fact that a major competitor now decided to take a hand in the game. Not only is it the world's biggest computer supplier, IBM is also a major manufacturer of computer chips in its own right. As well as buying Intel chips, it also makes its own. IBM now decided to announce that its investigations showed the fault to be more serious than Intel claimed and that it would not be shipping any more Pentium-based IBM computers until further notice.

This announcement was the prelude to major problems. The Attorneys General of Connecticut and Florida said they thought Intel's non-replacement policy might be a violation of their states' consumer protection laws. Big customers started deferring buying decisions until the mess was sorted out. Even TV chat-show host David Letterman made a Pentium joke on his show. Such jokes became common on the Internet. Sample: Why is the mathematical constant Pi such an irregular number (it is 3.1416)? Answer: It's really 3 but it was calculated on a Pentium.

It was the jokes that hurt most of all and that triggered Intel's decision to reverse its policy and offer to replace all Pentium chips for new ones. 'The essence of the announcement', said Jim Jarrett, 'was the policy change, an apology for our previous policy which had been perceived as arrogant, and an announcement that we would make a material reserve against fourth quarter earnings to cover replacement and associated costs.' In the event, this reserve came to $475 million.

Intel CEO Andy Groves summed up the problem when he observed, 'We didn't think that most people needed to replace their processors. They didn't like us making the decision for them. We approached replacement from an engineering point of view, when we should have treated it as a customer satisfaction issue.'

Intel seems to be genuinely convinced that the Pentium flaw was insignificant for most users and genuinely convinced that the furore was no more than a storm in a teacup – a media feeding frenzy deliberately exacerbated by IBM's decision to make capital out of their dilemma.

But in the end it wasn't the production flaw that cost Intel so much money: it was the company's decision to leave itself vulnerable to attacks from a competitor, damaging gossip on the Internet and jokes on network television. It was this that forced the share price down, not a one-in-nine-billion chance of a wrong digit.

What is especially instructive about Intel's case is that it was probably the first occasion in history when a major corporation was exposed via the Internet *and* when the corporation's chief executive attempted to counter the damage by using the Internet to appeal directly to users, over the heads of the media. Yet the attempt was unsuccessful, because it was based around traditional PR methods of soft-soap reassurance backed by technical-sounding scientific research. This failed because Intel was addressing the wrong problem. The issue was not whether the Pentium chip could be relied on: the issue was whether Intel and its statements could be relied on. In the event, the customers' actions showed that many of them did not trust Intel.

This case has highlighted how careful any corporation must be when dealing with consumer issues because customers are in immediate possession of all relevant information via the Internet (and possibly even more information than the company itself has).

More importantly, if the company makes any move that even appears to be evading its responsibility for its product, it will immediately forfeit credibility in *all* its statements – no matter whether they are true or not. The Intel experience showed that it is not enough for companies to *say* they are standing behind their products: they actually *have* to stand behind them, if they want their corporate image to survive.

One can compare the results of the Intel case with the case of the Hewlett-Packard Inkjet printer described in Chapter Sixteen. No one had to force Hewlett-Packard to put its hand in its pocket and spend millions of dollars rectifying a fault that was trivial but potentially damaging to its corporate image. H-P did it because it could foresee what the consequences might be if it didn't. Intel took a calculated chance that no one would notice there was a tiny problem – but someone did.

Moral: there will always be a Professor Nicely to play Nemesis to a product flaw, and there will always be the citizens of cyberspace to cry 'foul'.

CHAPTER SIX

GOOD AND FAITHFUL SERVANTS
How companies see their employees...*and how the Secret Service blew its own cover*

Companies are not normally beastly to their own employees on purpose. But just as it is common for a very powerful individual to be insensitive in dealing with others, so it is common for powerful corporations to fall into the trap of being insensitive in dealing with the men and women who work for them.

It is not that corporations are deliberately contemptuous of their own employees or carelessly undervalue them, but that they perceive their employees as being completely without power and hence not having any position of strength from which to negotiate. This is, of course, a mistaken point of view because in a free society with a free press, every individual has a position of strength: they can shop their employer to the media.

This pitfall entraps corporations much more frequently than it ought because powerful individuals, and corporations, intensely dislike making the discovery that the individual they thought harmless has in fact a sting after all. And they often respond to this unpleasant discovery by denying it altogether, like a maiden aunt refusing to be rattled by the wasps flying around the picnic sandwiches.

In the illustrative case described later, it was not merely one individual or organisation that became so intransigent but a whole series of them: Prime Minister Margaret Thatcher, at the zenith of her powers; the Secret Services, legendarily powerful and mysterious; the Cabinet Office, centre of Government authority; and the Civil Service, whose top officials are a byword for the effortless and efficient management of difficult problems. All were made to look foolish and incompetent by a single employee to whom they stubbornly refused to grant his full pension rights and who decided to hit back.

Human relationships are undoubtedly the thing that corporations are worst at, and which they too often get wrong. Frequently, this failing starts at the top and frequently, too, is a reflection of the failure of the corporation's own management to see and understand how they are perceived both by employees and by the outside world.

A recent case, involving Ford and its advertising agency, Ogilvy & Mather, showed how insensitive companies can be even on what every employer knows is potentially the most sensitive issue of all – that of employees' colour. In 1991, Ford's agency took a publicity photograph of workers at the company's Dagenham factory to be used in an advertising campaign for the Fiesta. Careful to be politically correct, the agency photographed people from every walk of life and every colour, including Afro-Caribbean and Indian as well as European. In 1995, the photograph surfaced again, this time in a Ford brochure and this time with four black faces changed into white ones. A Sikh employee had not only become white, but his turban had also disappeared.

Ford employees became angry at this racial censorship and complained to their union, the Transport and General Workers' Union (TGWU), who complained to management about the issue. To their credit, Ford immediately withdrew the brochure, wrote a letter of apology to the individuals concerned and paid them each a sum of money in compensation, blaming their agency for the error.

It was the explanation given by the agency, Ogilvy & Mather, which was especially revealing of what had really happened. The picture used in the second British brochure had been taken – unwittingly – from a doctored version that had been used in advertising campaigns for the Fiesta in Spanish and Polish markets, which have smaller Asian and black populations. It was for these markets that the unfamiliar black faces had been expunged – along with a crash dummy that was transformed into a moustachioed, Latin-looking mechanic.

63

As a Ford director said, the use of the picture was certainly not a malicious or racist action. Yet there is an insensitivity inherent in any corporate policy that feels free to change the facts, and change people's colour, simply as an expedient marketing tactic. To such companies, it is not the facts that matter: it is merely the appearance.

The *Daily Mail* got hot under the collar in its leader column and called the incident a 'crass and unforgivable blunder'. What is probably more worrying is that, far from being an event rare enough to merit an apoplectic editorial, the employees who conveniently changed colour are merely an outward symptom of how some large companies actually perceive their workforce in reality – faces in the crowd, merging one into another, and ultimately as interchangeable as motor spares. The people can be airbrushed as easily as the brochure pictures.

If this insensitivity resulted from a deliberate policy of treating people badly it might almost be preferable: at least one might hope to combat it and replace it with a more enlightened attitude. But when those who practise what might be called photo-racism do so without even realising it, then they are probably beyond reform.

How the Secret Service Blew its Own Cover

Officially, the Security Service (MI5) and the Secret Intelligence Service (MI6) don't do press or public relations. In reality, both organisations have in the past enjoyed the kind of PR image that would make most organisations green with envy.

From the second world war up to the 1980s, both organisations were synonymous with British cunning, courage, foresight and ingenuity. This real-life image gave rise to perhaps the most successful fictional character of all time, British secret agent 007, James Bond.

Partly this rosy picture grew out of the harmless fictions woven around the necessary secrecy of the intelligence world. Partly it was a legend leaked by serving and former officers of the services to their old chums in Fleet Street over lunch, in order to score a few PR points. And, partly, it was thanks to the pens of former intelligence officers, such as Graham

Greene, Dennis Wheatley, Ian Fleming and their creations, like the resourceful and redoubtable 007.

Looked at in one way, perhaps with a rather jaundiced eye, the intelligence services enjoyed for four decades the kind of conditions that the very worst commercial corporations would give their right arms for; the freedom to pull any dirty trick they pleased in complete secrecy and with the press and TV unable to report anything they found out about it. As if this wasn't advantage enough, the intelligence services were also able to manipulate the way their image filtered out to the press and public: if the press got hold of a story that made the services look good, then it would be confirmed by the simple expedient of not denying it – whether it was true or false. If the press got hold of a story that reflected badly on the services, then the story could have a 'D' notice slapped on it.

Given these competitive advantages – in effect, a kind of PR monopoly – even the world's worst organisations ought to enjoy the best corporate image possible.

No one can doubt that the secret, unpublished volumes of history of the two services must be filled with many, many records of individual heroism, self-sacrifice and brilliant planning, and both organisations must be congratulated for those successes. The sad thing is that while many successes remain secret, the blemishes in those secret histories should have been made public in the most dramatic way possible, because of an almost comically inept mishandling of one of the commonplace corporate situations – a disgruntled ex-employee.

Peter Wright was employed by the intelligence services from 1955 to 1976, rising to become Assistant Director of MI5. Because he was an expert in electronic communications and bugging (a kind of real-life Q) he was also intimately involved in many MI6 operations over two decades.[1]

No one has ever suggested that Wright was anything but a loyal, efficient and conscientious officer in the service, and dedicated to his country's security. Like all former officers of the services, he was expected to keep silent about everything he had seen and heard during his lifetime in intelligence.

However, when he retired in 1976, the service refused to give him a full pension. Wright had worked for 15 years for the Admiralty before joining MI5. He had been promised that his pension rights would be carried over to his intelligence service, something that happened in the cases of all subsequent scientists who joined MI5. In Wright's case, for some reason, the promise was not honoured and he left the service with only half a pension, a bureaucratic decision that was in Wright's own words, 'a bitter blow, and did much to sour my last few years in the Service'.[2]

Wright's response was to emigrate to Australia and, from the safety of a land beyond British jurisdiction, to dictate his memoirs for publication to the whole world in the form of his 1987 book *Spycatcher*.

In his book, dictated to and written by journalist Chapman Pincher, Wright made a number of damaging disclosures. He said that, 'For five years we bugged and burgled our way across London at the State's behest, while pompous bowler-hatted civil servants in Whitehall pretended to look the other way.'

He claimed that the CIA asked MI5 for technical assistance in assassinating leaders of third world countries; that MI5 bugged the embassies of both enemies and friends alike; and that a small clique of disgruntled officers in MI5 asked him to join their plan to de-stabilise the Labour government of Harold Wilson.[3]

The response from the British Government and Civil Service under Margaret Thatcher was almost farcical. First they tried to ban its publication in Australia and later in Britain, even though the book was already freely available over the counter in the United States and thousands of British people were ordering it by credit card over the telephone from New York book shops.

From a corporate image point of view, nothing could have been more ill-advised than this course of action, because it announced to the world that the British Government and its intelligence services were not seriously interested in keeping state secrets from the nation's potential enemies – merely that they wished to keep their own ineptitude secret from the British people.

Once this misguided strategy was adopted, its malevolent effects snowballed. Sir Robert Armstrong, the Cabinet Secretary and most senior civil servant in Britain, was sent over to stand in the witness box in an Australian court to give evidence as to why the book should be banned. Instead, under the full glare of the world's media, he was compelled by Wright's legal counsel to admit that he had been 'economical with the truth'.[4]

It is very clear that the *Spycatcher* mess could have been averted at any stage simply by giving Wright what most rational people accept he was entitled to: his pension rights. That he was not given this entitlement points to a deliberate refusal on the part of someone to appear to give in to pressure, and the 'someone' favoured by the press at the time was Margaret Thatcher.

Whoever took the decision, it was the wrong one. It led to the damaging, probably irrevocably, of decades of successful image-building by the intelligence services and showed them as bungling, short-sighted and less clever than their opponents. Equally it irrevocably further damaged the standing of Government because its most senior civil servant was exposed as untrustworthy and those composing the cabinet were shown to be incompetent negotiators, trying – and failing – to protect their own image.

It is hard to imagine that anyone in government would be so unwise as to repeat these mistakes, but just in case they are tempted, they would do well to remember the lessons of *Spycatcher*: if you treat your employees badly they will shop you to the press, whoever you are. Do not imagine that individuals are without power: it is the press and the Internet that gives them power.

All organisations, even those dedicated to secrecy, are actors in the see-through society. In the information age, even James Bond is powerless to stop the spread of information, electronically, globally, inevitably.

CHAPTER SEVEN

COMPANIES ON THE COUCH
How psychologists see companies…and how Lloyd's burnt its fingers

The idea of analysing the psychology of groups and organisations is far from new. Sigmund Freud devoted a book to 'group psychology' as long ago as 1921, while his most notable pupil, Carl Jung, coined the celebrated phrase 'collective unconscious'. The trouble with these well-turned phrases is that it is not clear how we are meant to take them. Are they simply useful metaphors or is there really such a thing as the 'collective unconscious', hanging around invisibly in the air, perhaps hovering over the conference table during board meetings?[1]

For the first half of this century, the tendency was for psychology not to take the idea of group behaviour or a group mind seriously in anything other than a metaphorical sense. But in the explosion of interest in experimental psychology in Britain and America that followed the second world war, psychology acquired its first experimental tools to measure and observe the dynamics of group behaviour. And what the new experiments showed was that these phrases are not simply metaphorical: they refer to measurably real and observable states of collective mind and forms of collective behaviour that do not occur in the individual alone.

Many people, including senior corporate executives, have great difficulty in accepting the reality of a group mind or group behaviour. Yet this is surprising when you consider how much concrete evidence of the existence of such entities there is to be commonly found within groups of all kinds. In organisations that have the capacity to retain their structure and persist for any length of time, the group's *esprit de corps* can and does persist despite the fact that its individual personnel change continually and may even turn over completely – as in an army regiment, a school or hospital, for example. People come and go, but the regime remains remarkably stable year in, year out, its traditions and prejudices intact, unless and until there is some periodic revolutionary change that imposes a new regime on the group.

There is a considerable body of academic work on this and many other aspects of the subject. The classic psychology text is Cartright and Zander's *Introduction to Group Dynamics* published in 1968. From the outset, its authors address the central issue: are groups and hence group psychology real entities or simply useful metaphors?

'There was never much doubt [in psychology] about the "existence" of individual organisms,' say the authors, 'but when attention turned to groups of people and to social institutions, a great confusion arose. Discussions of these matters invoked terms like "group mind", "collective representations", "collective unconscious" and "culture". And people argued heatedly as to whether such terms refer to any real phenomena or whether they are merely "abstractions" or "analogies". On the whole, the disciplines concerned with institutions (anthropology, economics, political science and sociology) have freely attributed concrete reality to supra-individual entities, whereas psychology with its interest in the physiological basis of behaviour, has been reluctant to admit existence to anything other than the behaviour of organisms.'[2]

Some researchers were thinking about organisations not merely in psychological terms, but in psychiatric terms, from the earliest days. Sigmund Freud published his 1921 book, *Group Psychology and the Analysis of the Ego*, in which he applied his whole theory of psychoanalysis to groups as distinct from individuals. Moreover, Freud's publication came immediately after two other similar and influential books on the same subject: Le Bon's *The Crowd: A Study of the Group Mind* and McDougall's *The Group Mind*, both published in Britain in 1920.[3,4]

But the subject really took off in the years immediately before and after the Second World War. The rise of fascist dictatorships in Europe had stimulated much academic interest in group behaviour and in 1945, Kurt Lewin, who had coined the phrase 'group dynamics', established the

Research Center for Group Dynamics at Massachusetts Institute of Technology.

Lewin was a German Jew who left Germany for the United States when the Nazis came to power in 1933. He spent two years at Cornell University and the next nine at the Iowa Child Research Station before moving to MIT. The list of students Lewin attracted during these years is a roll-call of some of the most distinguished names in experimental psychology in the post-war years, including Cartright and Zander, Festinger, Bavelas, Lippitt and anthropologist Margaret Mead.

One illuminating sidelight of the research conducted into group behaviour at this time is that it seems usually to be centred on the workers, rather than on those who direct the corporation. Turning, for instance, to the section of Cartright and Zander on 'Leadership and Performance of Group Functions', you find references to studies of schoolboys doing carpentry, of women working sewing machines in a pyjama factory (later improbably immortalised in song as the hit Broadway musical *The Pyjama Game*), of basketball teams, of bomber crews, of boy cadets in the Belgian Navy. But you will search in vain for studies of the group behaviour of factory owners, corporate executives, military brass, or even senior faculty members.

Of course, like everything else in life, this research has to be seen in the context of the time in which it was conducted, a cold war world that was still very authoritarian. The 'them and us' flavour of these studies reflects the social reality of the times. But it is hard to resist the conclusion that while those funding such studies were keen to find out what made the workers tick, there was much less enthusiasm for lifting the veil of such mysteries in the boardroom. Matters have changed little in the years since.

In Le Bon's book, which strongly influenced Freud, he says that the difference between individual and group behaviour is that the group has 'a sort of collective mind'. The group is a new 'provisional being' made up of each individual member (in today's Internet culture we would probably feel happy with the idea of a 'virtual mind'). Significantly, he also says that in the group, the distinctive consciousness of each individual is dropped, so that a kind of racial or collective unconscious emerges that forms the basis of the group's cohesion and action. Le Bon also believed that an important force at work in such a group is that of 'suggestibility'.[5]

Freud accepted the idea of the collective unconscious but not the idea of hypnotic suggestion; for who, he asked, was the hypnotist? Freud believed that the group's behaviour was voluntary, not the result of suggestion. He introduced the concept of libido to explain group behaviour: 'Libido is the energy of those instincts to do with all that may be comprised under the word "love".' Thus, according to Freud, the binding force of the group was the emotional ties of the members.

This is highly significant because, if true, it means that the fundamental dynamic of the corporation is not a rational purpose, as we usually like to think, but an emotional, non-rational one.

In his 1978 book, *The Psychoanalysis of Organisations*, Robert de Board of the Tavistock Institute summarised Freud's view thus:

* The major force operating in a group is the libido: the sexual instinct operating within every individual, which is basic to his behaviour and is not capable of further dissection. This does not mean or imply that group behaviour is sexual, in the usual meaning of the word. In the normal nature of things, the libido finds its most obvious expression in the sexual union of a man and woman. However, Freud said, 'in other circumstances, [the sexual instincts] are diverted from this aim or are prevented from reaching it, though always preserving enough of their original nature to keep their identity recognisable (as in the longing for proximity and self-sacrifice)'.

* The group is bound together through libidinal ties to the leader and to the other members of the group.

* The emotional bonds in the group derive essentially from 'identification', which Freud described as the earliest expression of an emotional tie with another person.

* The process of identification involves the 'introjection' of the admired or loved object into the ego ideal. In the group, this object is the leader with whom each member identifies, and having the object in their ego ideals, they can identify with each other.

71

* The leader of the group...is able to exercise his authority in the group because he is now the group ideal, each member having replaced his own ego with him. [6]

Even if Freud's theory were proved correct, however, one key issue remains unresolved. Surely many people, especially those experienced as senior executives within commercial organisations, would answer Freud's earlier question – who is the hypnotist that makes suggestions to the group? – as simply the group's leader. Isn't it the charismatic chief executive who takes all the tough decisions? Isn't it he or she who both directs the organisation through force of personality and gives it its essential character? Like Henry Ford; or Thomas Watson, legendary founder of IBM; or Winston Churchill? Bill Clinton or Tony Blair?

In fact, more recent studies suggest that Freud was quite correct: that there is no 'hypnotist' who directs the group, and that even charismatic leaders are prisoners of their own organisations.

In *The Psychoanalysis of Organisations*, Robert de Board writes about the third major influence on the theory of group and organisational behaviour alongside Freud and Lewin – British psychiatrist Wilfred Bion. Bion worked at London's Tavistock Institute of Human Relations and conducted a long series of group studies in the 1950s and 1960s (his papers were published in 1968). From his early experiments, Bion reached several basic conclusions, which include:

* Individual psychology is fundamentally group psychology. Behaviour by one member of the group influences, and is influenced by, all the other members.

* The rational working of a group is profoundly affected by the emotions and irrational feelings of its members. The full potential of the group is only realised when this fact is recognised and dealt with.

* Administrative and managerial problems are simultaneously personal and interpersonal problems expressed in organisational terms. [7]

From his experiments, Bion concluded that an organisation or group works at two different levels, just as Freud had said the individual works. There is, said Bion, an emotional level of the group that results in certain basic assumptions of its members, and then there is the 'real' or working aim of the group, that which it consciously focuses on.

De Board explains that, 'According to Bion, there are three distinct emotional states of groups from which three basic assumptions can be deduced. Only one basic assumption will be evidenced at any one time, although it can change three or four times in an hour or persist for three months.'

The three basic assumptions, or underlying forms of group emotion, are: Dependency, where the group has formed around a leader for protection and direction; Pairing, where the group has formed in order to create a new, as yet unborn leader; and Fight-Flight, where the group has met to fight a threat or run away from it.

If, for instance, the underlying emotional assumption of a group is Fight-Flight, then it will ignore all other activities or try to suppress or avoid them. In this kind of group the leader must be prepared to lead the group against a common 'enemy'.

At the working group level, however, whether it is a small group like a committee or a large one like the Army, there is a specific, overt task to perform. To achieve this, the members of the group have to co-operate and use a sophisticated approach, organising formal administrative structures. Formal rational methods are consciously employed to achieve the group's goal.

According to le Board, 'Underlying [Bion's] concept of the work group and the basic assumption groups is basic Freudian theory. The group, when it is working rationally and co-operatively, is like the ego, mediating between reality and self.

'Like the ego, the work group can be influenced and, at times, overwhelmed by emotions arising from unconscious processes.'

Perhaps most interesting of all in Bion's scheme is the answer to the question: isn't it the leader who leads? Says Robert de Board: 'The person who accepts the role of leader in a Fight-Flight group must be prepared to lead the group against the common enemy and, where this does not

73

exist, to create one. He is expected to recognise danger and enemies, and spur on his followers to courage and self-sacrifice. However, this leadership is based on paranoia: "they" are endangering the group; "they", wholly evil, have to be attacked and destroyed. Once the danger is past, the leader is ignored and any statement by him that does not involve fight or flight is also ignored. In Bion's concept, such a leader is entirely the creature of the group: "the leader has no greater freedom to be himself than any other member of the group".'

The man or woman chosen to be chief executive is chosen to meet the needs of the moment, the corporation's currently perceived situation in the market: to protect and consolidate when things are going well; to facilitate the emergence of a new leader when evolution is called for; or to fight off the corporation's enemies when competition is perceived to be tough.

Are there any specific ways in which the nature of group behaviour can cause the senior executives of a company to behave in a manner that they would not normally behave as individuals? In other words, does working for a corporation make people behave differently? The evidence from experimental psychology is that it does.

Solomon Asch performed a ground-breaking experiment in the 1960s. He brought college students into the laboratory apparently to participate in an experiment on visual perception. The group's task was ostensibly to make a series of judgements in which they compared the length of a drawing of a given vertical line with three other lines and decided visually which matched. Each student was asked in turn to say which of three comparison lines most closely matched the given line.

In reality, only one student in each group was a naïve subject. The others had all been primed to choose unanimously a line that was obviously wrong. The real purpose of the experiment was to determine whether the naïve subjects would believe the evidence of their own eyes? Or whether they would conform to the majority verdict by choosing a match that is obviously wrong?

Asch found that three-quarters of the subjects yielded to the unanimous judgement of the others on at least one trial and that one-third yielded on at least half the trials.

Care was taken in the experiment to ensure that the experimental subjects did not personally know the other participants, and the other participants were instructed not to attempt to coerce or influence the subject's behaviour in any way. Even so, the experiment clearly showed that, once we are part of a group, many of us make wrong decisions that we do not make alone.

In one sense it is a banal observation that people in groups tend to agree with the consensus of opinion. Yet most senior executives would be indignant to be told that many of their boardroom decisions were not truly independent. Once more, it is the corporate unconscious that is deciding the company's actions and decisions, rather than the rational conscious processes that managers prefer to imagine govern their behaviour.

Of course, no theory of group psychology can take into account the many different unconscious motives of the individuals who join an organisation, just as no purely personal psychology can say what kind of neuroses the individual's personal history might lead to. But the kind of group unconscious the organisation evolves is not arbitrary: it is dependent on the dynamics of group psychology.

This finding, that organisations such as commercial corporations really do have an unconscious mind, and that, 'like the ego, the work group can be influenced and, at times, overwhelmed by emotions arising from unconscious processes'[8] has profound implications for anyone who wishes to understand corporate behaviour.

Most people have heard the famous story of the riddle of the Sphinx. The strange beast, who Oedipus met on his journey, asked: 'What is it that walks on four legs in the morning, two legs in the afternoon and three legs in the evening?' To which Oedipus was able to reply correctly, 'Man himself'.

American psychoanalyst, Martin Rioch, has updated the question for today's corporate culture: 'If the Sphinx were to ask "What is it that on Monday is wrangling, cruel and greedy; on Tuesday is indifferent and lazy; on Wednesday is effectively and intelligently collaborative?" one could easily answer, "That is man and it is also man in the group".'

This conclusion suggests, too, that like individuals, companies can behave in an aberrant way because of motivating forces of which they are not even aware; that, like individuals, companies can become neurotic, and even psychotic under certain circumstances.

How Lloyd's Burnt its Fingers

The Yale School of Organisation and Management has predicted that over the next 25 years there are likely to be some 200,000 deaths around the world due to the effects of asbestos. The legal claims made by these unfortunate people will cost the asbestos manufacturers some $50,000 million – ten times the combined net assets of the asbestos companies and totalling about the same as the entire assets of the US liability insurance industry.

When this financial maelstrom comes about, or even only a fraction of it, the bills will be paid ultimately not by the giant corporations who have caused the hazard or by the companies who traded in asbestos products. The bills will land ultimately on the doormats of doctors, dentists, farmers, pilots, lawyers, retired businessmen, sports people and a dozen other professions, living around Britain – many of them more or less ordinary well-off people who have pledged unlimited liability to become external 'Names' at Lloyd's.

In the past five years, hundreds of these people have already been financially ruined as their pledge of unlimited liability has been called on by the Lloyd's committee to meet escalating losses incurred through the underwriting of risks, which seemed remote at the time the premiums were paid but have since come horribly true.[9]

The main source of these claims has been the awarding of damages in the courtroom to victims of industrial diseases, such as asbestosis, and environmental damage caused by industrial processes. There have, too, been unpredictable and unexpected disasters, such as the tragic explosion aboard the Piper Alpha oil platform and a series of hurricanes whose girlish names conceal devastation costing thousands of millions. But the main impact on Lloyd's has been the acceptance in courts in

America and Britain that corporations are financially liable for the damage they cause.

The principal cause of this human and financial disaster, the case of asbestosis, demonstrates all too clearly people behaving as a group in ways that it is hard to imagine they would ever have behaved as individuals.

It has been well known and understood for almost a century that asbestos causes lung disease. Reports from factory inspectors as long ago as 1898 pointed out the problem. A report by the US Bureau of Labor, published in 1918, drew attention to premature deaths among asbestos workers and the fact that some insurance companies were refusing to sell them life insurance because of their occupation.

It was an article by Dr E W Cooke in the *British Medical Journal* in 1924 on the death of a textile factory worker, Nellie Kershaw, which led to the disease of asbestosis being formally recognised. One particularly unpleasant aspect of the disease is that it can take decades to develop and show itself and can be contracted even after only brief exposure to asbestos fibres.

America's largest insurance company, Metropolitan Life, conducted a study of health conditions in asbestos textile mills on behalf of the asbestos producers between 1929 and 1931. The study highlighted the risks run by workers and found that more than half of the 126 people examined had developed asbestosis. Its report to the asbestos manufacturers told them squarely they must 'seriously face the problem of dust control in asbestos plants'.

The asbestos producers, led by the largest manufacturer, Johns-Manville, managed to suppress the report until 1935 when it was published in censored form to minimise the damage to their businesses.

The next forty years were a tragic story of the asbestos companies making large profits from asbestos, and suppressing medical information while their employees contracted and slowly died from asbestosis.

Because the asbestos manufacturers knew that their factories had created an industrial health hazard, making them potentially liable to legal damages, they jointly campaigned to establish voluntary compensation schemes on a 'no fault' basis. By this means, they were able

77

to get away with providing inadequate financial compensation while at the same time preventing victims of asbestosis from suing their employers in the courts.

According to Adam Raphael in his book on the Lloyd's affair, *Ultimate Risk*: 'The legal barriers against actions for negligence proved remarkably successful. By the late 1950s, the manufacturers and their insurers had paid only minute amounts of damages, with most claimants receiving as little as $5,000 a head in workman's compensation. All this time the use of the mineral was expanding fast.'[10]

Although the manufacturers closed their eyes and ears to the health dangers of asbestos, medical research continued. Dr Kenneth Smith worked for the largest US manufacturer, Johns-Manville. He conducted a study of 700 workers at a Canadian plant in 1948 and could find only four with healthy lungs – the rest all had some degree of asbestosis. Dr Smith reported to his employers but was told that it was company policy not to inform the employees of their illness.

Johns-Manville's vice president for production explained, 'They have not been told of this diagnosis, for it is felt that as long as the man feels well, is happy at home and at work, and his physical condition remains good, nothing should be said... The fibrosis of this disease is irreversible and permanent so that eventually compensation will be paid to each of these men. But as long as the man is not disabled, it is felt he should not be told of his condition so that he can live and work in peace and the Company can benefit by his many years of experience. Should the man be told of his condition today, there is a very definite possibility that he would become mentally and physically ill, simply through the knowledge that he has the disease.'[11]

This chilling admission was not an isolated instance. Charles Roemer later recalled a conversation he had with Vandivier Brown, Johns-Manville's attorney and brother of the company's president, Louis Brown. Roemer said that Vandivier Brown called another asbestos manufacturer, Unarco, 'a bunch of fools' for telling their employees that they had contracted asbestosis. Roemer replied: 'Mr Brown, do you mean to tell me that you would let them work until they dropped dead?' To which Brown replied, 'Yes. We save a lot of money that way.'[12]

Nemesis overtook the asbestos industry in October 1964. At a press conference in New York, Dr Irving Selikoff, director of the environmental sciences laboratory of the Mount Sinai School of Medicine, told the world's press what the manufacturers had known for decades: that asbestos was deadly.

Working with union officials, Dr Selikoff conducted tests on more than 1,000 workers in insulation factories. He found that 87 per cent of those exposed to asbestos dust for more than twenty years had severe and irreversible lung damage. A second study found that asbestos insulation workers were seven times more likely to die from lung cancer and three times more likely to die from stomach cancer than other industrial workers.

By itself, the dramatic publicity might not have stimulated change, but there were also changes taking place in the legal system. Until the 1960s the liability of manufacturers for their products was interpreted in a very narrow way. In the wake of greater concern over consumer protection issues, the law was extended to cases in which 'the defective condition of the product makes it unreasonably dangerous to the user'.

Under these reforms the first lawsuits were brought against asbestos firms and resulted in the award of massive damages.

Clarence Borel, the first litigant, was an asbestos worker aged 53 whose widow sued Johns-Manville, Pittsburgh Corning and Eagle-Pitcher in 1969. Borel's widow won damages of $79,000. In their defence the companies protested that no one knew the potential danger to insulation workers until Dr Selikoff's study in 1964, but the plaintiffs were able to show that the companies had known of the dangers for decades.

As time went by and the cases piled up, juries awarded higher and higher damages against the companies. In 1981, Johns-Manville had to pay $500,000 damages to the widow of Edward Moran. A year later, a retired boiler maker, James Cavett, won damages of $2.3 million. A South Carolina lawyer, Ronald Motley, described Johns-Manville as 'the greatest corporate mass murderer in history'.

Within months, Johns-Manville filed under Chapter 11 of the Federal Bankruptcy Code for protection against its creditors and shortly after collapsed, insolvent. More than 16,000 claims had been filed against the company and it had paid out hundreds of millions in compensation.

A similar pattern of events had taken place in Britain in the factories of Britain's biggest asbestos maker, Turner and Newall, who today call themselves T&N. The subject of Dr Cooke's 1924 paper in the *British Medical Journal* was a 33-year-old asbestos weaver called Nellie Kershaw, who worked for Turner Brothers Asbestos Company from the age of 13.

When Miss Kershaw died, Turner Brothers wrote to their insurers, 'We feel that it will be exceedingly dangerous to admit any liability whatever in such a case and before referring the matter to you, we considered that we ought to do all in our power to repudiate the claim.'[13]

Following Nellie Kershaw's death and Dr Cooke's findings, a study was conducted of Turner and Newall's Rochdale factory. It found that one in four of the workers had lung damage through asbestos. In 1931, the Home Office introduced new regulations requiring the use of extractor fans in all plants wherever workers were exposed to asbestos dust on more than an occasional basis. The regulations defined 'occasional' as once a week – meaning that the manufacturers would have to install fans extensively.

The firm's founder, Mr Turner, wrote to his partner, Mr Newall, 'I feel this definition of "occasional" is rather too strict. We must take a small risk by stretching the regulations for our own ends.'[14]

In 1954, Turner and Newall commissioned the eminent epidemiologist, Professor Richard Doll, to conduct a scientific study of the health of asbestos workers. Doll's findings were unequivocal and his conclusions uncompromising: asbestos workers were ten times more likely to contract lung cancer than other workers. The company tried to suppress Doll's report. Its medical director, Dr John Knox, wrote to Doll asking him to suppress his findings as the company's management had decided that 'the conclusions reached were not supported by medical evidence'. Professor Doll was outraged by this and subsequently published the report himself.

Further echoes of the response by American manufacturers were to be found in the case of Charlie Coyle, an asbestos insulation worker in the Clyde shipyards who contracted asbestosis. Attempts by his lawyers to press a claim for compensation were continually delayed. The delay was not merely incompetence. Turner and Newall's lawyers had written to the board: 'The man has a very poor expectation of life. And, if he does succumb, the claim will not be any more expensive and without his evidence the solicitors will be in greater difficulties. In short, I do not think tactically we have anything to lose by leaving the matter in abeyance.'[15]

The malign effects of this deadly industry travelled far beyond the asbestos companies themselves and were passed on like a corporate contagion to the insurers of industrial risks, principally the Lloyd's market. In an echo of the asbestos companies' own defence, it was later to be claimed that no one outside the asbestos industry itself, including the medical profession, knew about the impending disaster that asbestosis claims represented in the 1970s or early 1980s. But some individuals, at least, had taken the trouble to inform themselves and hence were forearmed.

Adam Raphael wrote that 'some underwriters were more far-sighted than others. Roger Bradley, a Janson Green underwriter, recalls a conversation in October 1973 with Sturge's leading non-marine underwriter, Ralph Rokeby-Johnson. In the course of an amiable game of golf at Walton Heath, Bradley was taken aback when asked by Rokeby-Johnson: "Has Green [Peter Green] got his asbestos reinsurance in place and has he got enough of it?" When he asked what that meant he was startled by the reply: "What I can tell you, my friend, is that asbestosis is going to change the wealth of nations. Lloyd's will probably be bankrupted in the final chapter unless something happens to intervene." Pressed further Rokeby-Johnson predicted that asbestos claims would result in losses rising to $120 billion by the end of the century. It turned out to be a remarkably prescient forecast, as the most authoritative estimates now suggest that asbestos will cost insurers $50–$100 billion.'

It was late 1980 before Lloyd's became officially worried about asbestos and set up the Asbestos Working Party to co-ordinate information about the hole Lloyd's had found itself in.

According to Adam Raphael, 'Its first chairman was Ted Nelson, a non-marine underwriter, and it included other leading market figures on long-tail syndicates, such as Charles Skey of syndicate 219, Ralph Rokeby-Johnson of Sturge syndicate 210, Robin Jackson of Merrett and Don Tayler, underwriter for Pulbrook syndicate 90. This later led to bitter accusations that underwriters on the working party had used inside information to safeguard their own position by taking out reinsurance policies covering their asbestos liabilities from other less well-informed underwriters in the market.'

Five years later, the ominous predictions of the well-informed few had started to come true. Names – the well-off individuals who pledge their wealth to underwrite insurance risks and who normally expected to receive a profits cheque once a year – were starting to get bills instead. Doctors, dentists and farmers were receiving demands for £500,000, £1 million, £1,500,000, all to cover the ballooning cost of asbestosis and other legal awards.

It is illuminating, Adam Raphael points out, to compare what happened when the malign hand of the asbestos industry touched Lloyd's in the 1980s with how the organisation had reacted to a similar crisis a hundred years earlier.

In 1870, the steamer *Venezuelan*, on route from Barbados to Liverpool was disabled, losing her rudder. Luckily, the passengers and some crew members were rescued by another ship, which took them on to New York. Here the story became embroidered by the press and the *New York Herald* ran a sensational story under the headline: MID-OCEAN HORROR – a story picked up and run by the *Liverpool Courier*. Things looked black for the *Venezuelan* and at Lloyd's the chances of a total loss seemed so probable that the premium demanded shot up to 50 per cent.

However, the owner, A B Forwood, who was also an underwriting member of Lloyd's, received a letter from the captain saying that the press reports were exaggerated; the ship was basically sound and was very likely to make it safely to port. Finding himself in possession of this useful inside information, Forwood decided to make a little easy money. He sent a telegram to his London agent instructing him to underwrite £1,000, thus making a virtually risk-free killing of £500.

This piece of insider trading infuriated the Lloyd's committee so much when they learned of it, that they set up an enquiry, found him guilty and expelled him. In fact, the society was later found to be exceeding its powers and was compelled to reform its constitution to enable it to outlaw sharp practice of this sort.

But the sense of outrage was unmistakable. Members should not use inside knowledge to enrich themselves at the expense of others, believed the committee of 1870; the market should be open and fair for all. One member should not take advantage of another.

A little more than a hundred years later, the asbestosis scandal broke. In 1980, the Asbestosis Working Party was formed. In 1982 nearly 50 policies were written in what is called the run-off market (which involved asbestos) by a syndicate headed by a prominent underwriter, Richard Outhwaite.

'The run-off premiums proved to be completely inadequate for the risks that were being carried,' wrote Adam Raphael, 'the policies turned out to be the most disastrous insurance deals ever written at Lloyd's. Within five years, Outhwaite's Names had had to pay calls of more than 100 per cent, and the sum of known claims was nearer 1,000 per cent.'

Richard Outhwaite was castigated for incompetence but was defended by John Donner, chairman of Donner Underwriting Agencies, who said, 'I have never used the word conspiracy but what I do say is that information which was privy to a handful of people at the very top of Lloyd's was not properly disseminated.'

According to Adam Raphael, 'At the centre of his suspicions was the role of the Asbestos Working Party. Its members, he believed, had taken advantage of their inside knowledge of the developing asbestos crisis to transfer their syndicates' outstanding liability to Outhwaite.'

Donner's allegations reverberated around the high-tech glass and steel Lloyd's building designed by Richard Rogers, and its anachronistic mahogany-panelled boardroom, designed generations before by John Adam, and carefully rebuilt. Which would respond? The cruel modernity of glass and steel? Or the humanistic tradition of mahogany panelling?

Lloyd's appointed four members of its council to consider the Donner allegations: Sir Maurice Hodgson, former chairman of ICI; Matthew Patient, a partner in Coopers & Lybrand Deloitte; David Walker, chairman of the securities and investment board; and Alan Lord, deputy chairman and chief executive of Lloyd's.

Six months later, the four dismissed Donner's allegations and concluded that a formal investigation was not warranted because 'no evidence has been provided which supports the suggestion that in placing their contracts the underwriters took advantage of information which was available to the AWP but was not made available to the market'.

The allegations, however, did not go away. The Lloyd's Names Associations' Working Party, the organisation formed by the Names to fight their case, later claimed that Lloyd's insiders had deliberately withheld information from Names in order to lure them into the market. 'Since 1979,' said the working party, 'nearly 10,000 Names have joined Lloyd's while successive Chairmen and Committee members knew that asbestos could break Lloyd's.'

The working party's chairman, Christopher Stockwell, said, 'What happened in 1982 was a disgraceful cover-up. Information known to Lloyd's was withheld from the external Names.'

During the eight years to 1990, a member of Lloyd's council who underwrote a standard 'line' of £400,000 made an average profit of £72,400 from his syndicates. An underwriter made an average profit of £64,000, while a director of a managing or members' agent made a profit of £40,800. An external name, by contrast, made a loss of £11,200.

The angry cries of aggrieved Names were answered only by the glass and steel of the 1990s: their voices went unheeded in the carefully preserved mahogany boardroom.

CHAPTER EIGHT

IT'S MY PARTY AND I'LL CRY IF I WANT TO

How companies become neurotic...*and how IBM fumbled the PC market*

Neurosis in people is commonly accompanied by anxiety: the constant worry over job, marriage, health, mortgage, children, schools, and a hundred other unpredictable aspects of life. Large companies rarely suffer from this kind of anxiety, because large companies very rarely go under. As individuals, we worry lest the worst happens: for corporations, the worst never happens – even when the worst happens.

When securities trader Nick Leeson gambled away the entire cash reserves of Barings Bank, the bank remained intact and was bought for its reputation, its contacts, and its profit-making capability by a Dutch bank for £1. As far as the directors were concerned, it was business as usual – they even kept their six-figure bonuses.

Corporations only start to behave neurotically in an obvious way when competitive pressures expose their weaknesses, when their marketing plans fail, when smarter, quicker competitors make them look foolish, or when they start to think they are being ganged up on.

More worrying perhaps is when their neurotic behaviour stems from deep flaws in the corporate personality; flaws that are normally buried deep under layers of protective camouflage but which can erupt again when a sore spot on the corporate hide is rubbed the wrong way, or when the company is faced with a task that calls for more moral courage than it can muster, and its weakness begins to show.

The symptoms of this kind of behaviour are not difficult to discern in the neurotic company. One test that almost never fails is to examine closely the annual report of a company that you know has come under fire in the press during the year, to see how the company has dealt with its problems. Has it swept them under the carpet? Or has it faced them squarely?

Common methods of weaselling out of problems are to minimise them by glossing over them with PR-speak, or to put them under wraps completely, for instance by claiming that they cannot be discussed because they are the subject of actual or possible legal action.

What this kind of behaviour really means is that the company has such a weak self-image it feels it has to manage the information that it makes available by pre-digesting it, so that the outside world knows what conclusion to arrive at: it cannot risk allowing people to make up their own minds about the facts.

Another even more common form of corporate neurosis arises when companies are thwarted in their plans to exploit the marketplace, perhaps because they are beaten by a smarter, nimbler competitor or because the market stubbornly refuses to behave in the way that the company thinks it will. When this happens, the neurotic company tends to stamp its foot and burst into the corporate equivalent of tears. This tearful outburst is often accompanied by a spending spree in the marketing department to try to restore the corporate good humour.

How IBM Fumbled the PC Market

There is an old joke in the Information Technology industry: How do you make a small fortune out of computers? Answer: You start with a large fortune. For IBM, the joke became a hard reality in 1992 when, in a single year, what was once the world's most profitable company turned in a loss of $4,970 million, the biggest annual loss in American corporate history.

The fall was a hard one. International Business Machines had for decades been a byword for corporate efficiency and success. IBM more than almost any other American corporation embodied in the public imagination the qualities of enterprise, innovation, efficiency and service.

Behind the corporate image façade, however, the company had been sickening for many years.

IBM's core problem was the same problem suffered by all successful empires: those in power refused to make any room for the next generation and acted to stifle any innovation that would dispossess them of their power. In IBM's case, those in power were the overwhelmingly successful mainframe barons who had grown rich on big expensive machines with proprietary architectures and expensive proprietary software in the 1970s and 1980s. The hardware and software, bought by practically all the world's largest corporations, were backed by a legendary quality of service and support. If anything went wrong with your IBM mainframe system, a team of red-hot technicians was on your doorstep within hours to fix it.[1]

This marketing strategy – demanding and getting a premium price for the IBM name because it symbolised quality of service – worked for far longer than it should have done simply because the customers, who were mainly other large companies who wanted to be like IBM themselves, felt safe with IBM and were reluctant to trust their computing to anyone else. If you are going to spend anything up to £10 million or more on hardware and software, you want to spend it with someone you can depend on – even if it means that you will be locked into their proprietary designs, and find it difficult to change to another supplier.

But although it had its customers' unconscious fears working in its favour, almost everything else in the market was working against IBM.

In the late 1970s, computers were getting smaller, more powerful and a lot cheaper. Apple, Commodore, Tandy and other manufacturers developed and introduced Personal Computers, selling in the high street for just a few thousand dollars. Some of the more entrepreneurial big computer manufacturers, like General Automation, were experimenting with PCs for corporate clients. Customers were demanding 'open' architectures that didn't lock them into one supplier. IBM started to feel the pinch of competition, first from minicomputers and later from PCs.

Hardware was also becoming much more reliable, so that service and support was becoming less of an issue. In any case, as its markets began

87

to be squeezed and profits dwindled, IBM was less and less able to afford to provide its legendarily high levels of support anyway.

Many individuals and groups within the corporation tried to get IBM started down the roads of open architecture and smaller machines, but they were usually strangled at birth by the mainframe barons, if it appeared that they might represent any serious internal competition.

Part of the problem, too, was that IBM has always tended to be an imitative, rather than an innovative company. When I first gained admittance to the company's famed UK research laboratory in 1975, I was surprised to find the only serious work in evidence was a team who were 'reverse engineering' – the polite phrase for taking to pieces – a word processor from the then market leader, Wang, in order to study its features.

Although the PC is closely identified with IBM's name, it was not an IBM innovation at all, simply a design the company, and others, copied from its inventor, Texan maverick Chuck Peddle. The PC operating system that sits on a 100 million desks around the world was also not written by IBM (perhaps surprising when you recall that, at the time of the PC's inception, IBM was by far the world's largest software house) but was created by Bill Gates and his embryonic Microsoft team, under contract to IBM.

Where IBM does get the credit is for taking an idea whose time had come, engineering it well and turning it into a universal standard by superb marketing. So successful was IBM that all the major corporate organisations that had bought its mainframes, also bought its desktop machines as replacements for typewriters. It was IBM marketing wizards who coined the term 'word processing'.

When it was launched in 1982, orders for the PC far outstripped the production capacity of the firm's Boca Raton factory. By the first five months of 1983, the Boca Raton plant was turning out PCs in astounding numbers, and at a rate that increased every day.

But despite this phenomenal success, the IBM PC, and its successor machine, the IBM AT, contained the seeds of their own downfall. Because IBM's PC division had designed the machine in record time using standard parts they bought in, they had broken the company's cardinal rule and created an open industry standard that could be copied in exact detail by any other electronics manufacturer. And it was here that IBM's problems began. As soon as it had opened up the corporate PC market, clone makers sprang up overnight wherever labour was cheap and factories were unburdened by unions or anti-pollution regulations. Soon, IBM's customers were able to buy PC machines that looked the same, performed the same, but cost half the price or less. Before long, they were performing better than IBM's at half the price.

Just as IBM itself had copied Chuck Peddle, so IBM in turn was copied by the cut-price manufacturers of the Pacific Rim. There was no patent or copyright in the PC design, no way of stopping these competitors swarming all over the market that IBM had pioneered. At the same time, it was obvious that the PC was going to play an increasingly significant role in corporate computing in the future, as the mainframe and minicomputer diminished in importance and the era of desktop computing arrived, and that there was plenty of money still to be made out of PCs by a clever player.

The bitterest blow was that IBM's most successful competitor was not one of the treacherous foreign devils of the Pacific Rim but a home-grown Texan company, Compaq, who consistently beat IBM into second place in its own market.

When it lost control of the Personal Computer market it had created, IBM reacted in what seemed on the surface a perfectly rational way. It sought to regain control of the market through its technical mastery by devising a patent hardware technology, called the 'Microchannel Architecture', which no other manufacturers could imitate except under license, and also by producing its own operating system, OS/2, which it claimed was better than Microsoft's software. It even sought to change the name of the PC, calling its new system the PS/2.

The key point about IBM's strategy in the PC market is that it was an attempt to re-run its successful strategy from the mainframe market. The company was again trading on its legendary quality of service: major corporate buyers of PCs would continue to buy the IBM name because of the hardware reliability and technical superiority that went with it – and would continue to pay a healthy premium price for those benefits. But they would also pay the price of becoming locked into IBM's proprietary designs once again.

At the same time, though, IBM started cost-cutting by taking much of its manufacturing offshore to low cost areas such as Korea and Italy, for components such as video screens and the PS/2 mouse, in order to get its prices as low as possible.

The reality was that Microchannel Architecture gave no perceptible performance advantage while denying users industry standard compatibility. If you bought a PC clone from the Far East, you could buy add-on cards to fit inside for relatively small sums. For example, you could buy a plug-in modem card to communicate with a remote computer for around £100, because there were scores of manufacturers of such cards competing in the market. For IBM's PS/2 machines, a plug-in modem card would cost £500 or more, because only a tiny handful of manufacturers were licensed by IBM to produce cards compatible with the Microchannel Architecture. Much the same was true of software. Users chose Microsoft's Windows over OS/2 because they preferred it, or more simply, because it was already installed on the PCs they bought.[2]

The company's move to offshore manufacturing meant that its hardware was no more reliable than other hardware available. Indeed, grumbles began to be heard that components like screens and 'mice' seemed to be prone to failure.

From a purely manufacturing and sales point of view, IBM's strategy seemed to make perfect sense. But it overlooked the fact that the big corporate PC buyers would find that they could buy hardware, software and service cheaper and better elsewhere, and that once those customers had gone, they were gone for good. The outcome of the strategy was disastrous.

IBM discovered that it wasn't trading on its reputation – it was selling the family silver.[3]

The sales figures tell what happened. In 1984, IBM had 63 per cent of the world PC market. By 1987 this had dropped to 38 per cent; by 1991 to just over 14 per cent (about the same share as the relatively tiny Apple); and by 1992 – the year of its biggest financial loss – to just 10.9

per cent. The majority of people didn't want IBM's PS/2 or its operating system: they were happy with PC clones.

It was when things started to go wrong that IBM reacted in the neurotic way that some large organisations do when under threat: it started spending big sums on advertising and public relations to try to prove to the world and to itself that its strategy was the correct one. IBM's PC division had three costly video films made on the new Microchannel Architecture and OS/2, and mailed tapes of these free of charge, unsolicited, to tens of thousands of PC users.

The subtitling staff of the PR department had clearly been working overtime and consuming many pots of coffee. The videos bore titles like: 'Tomorrow's Architecture Today', and 'The Way Forward' – stirring stuff, reminiscent of wartime Ministry of Information films about beating the enemy and pulling together. The problem was that they were mailing the videos to people who had already bought PS/2 machines, and hence preaching to the converted. And, in any case, the message was misdirected: it was IBM that had to pull together to defeat its enemies – not its customers.

Millions of pounds worth of newspaper, magazine and television advertising was booked. Many users ignored the videotapes and the adverts for the same reason that they had ignored the products – they had already chosen cheaper competitive products.

IBM's case is instructive because it not only involves one of the world's smartest marketing organisations making the wrong moves and sending out the wrong messages to its customers, it also provides a classic example of an unconsciously motivated corporate reaction that is commonplace when any board's predictions and plans fail. This reaction to the failure of prophecy is examined in detail in Chapter Fourteen. It is marked by an increased, almost religious fervour in the belief that has been proved wrong and in frantic attempts to proselytise more converts to the cause.

It is most often encountered in military organisations, where it is usually called 'reinforcing failure'. It is the unconscious motivating force that compelled generals on the western front in 1914–18 to continue to pour men and guns into battles that had long ago bogged down in the mud with no hope of victory.[4]

The lesson that is usually drawn from IBM's high profile failure is the importance of avoiding corporate arrogance. This is no doubt a valuable lesson for any company but, like most of the other cases discussed in this book, it was not the principal cause of IBM's failure. Anyone can misread the signs of impending defeat; anyone can misread the need to retreat and regroup. But only someone who is neurotically deluding themselves can continue to squander their irreplaceable assets reinforcing failure when the battle is over and the victors have already carried off the spoils.

IBM's behaviour is self-deluding but still understandable: one can almost sympathise with its emotional plight, having fallen from such a great height so quickly. But the behaviour of some corporations is occasionally so bizarre as to be not merely self-defeating but almost suicidal.

CHAPTER NINE

THE CRUEL WORLD OF WOOLLY JUMPERS

How companies go completely off the rails...and how Benetton alienated its customers

If some companies become neurotic to a greater or lesser extent, there are a few who go completely off their trolleys: their behaviour becomes so unpredictable, so bizarre, and so unrelated to their normal business practices that one can only compare it with that of an individual who has gone insane.

Of course, periodic bouts of communal insanity are not unknown in the animal and human population: March hares, lemmings and ladies' hats at Ascot spring to mind. True, companies do not usually leap into the sea or dress in bizarre hats but there are occasions when their actions can only be interpreted as some kind of primary mental aberration.

Probably the most important indicator of corporate insanity is when an organisation begins to behave in a way that is seriously self-defeating of its own long-term aims and welfare; when it tries to inflict harm on itself. Most companies occasionally do barmy things, just as most individuals occasionally trip up or lash out under pressure. But a few companies sometimes demonstrate behaviour that in any human individual would call for a strait-jacket and a spell in a padded room.

In general, one might say that, since it is every commercial organisation's primary aim to earn revenue by attracting customers, then any behaviour that diminishes revenue by driving customers away can be seen as a form of corporate insanity.

How Benetton Alienated its Customers

People walking or riding through the streets of London and other cities in 1989 were stunned to see huge, newly-posted 48-sheet advertisement hoardings that portrayed a blood-smeared newborn baby, a young man dying from AIDS and other grittily realistic photographs with emotionally disturbing content. What on earth were these posters advertising? A new fly-on-the-wall TV documentary? A shocking newspaper investigation into the plight of sick people?

It turned out that the photographs were the opening salvo in an advertising campaign by an Italian manufacturer of casual clothes, Benetton, and that the aim of the harrowing pictures was not to prick our social conscience but to persuade us to buy more woolly jumpers.[1]

Over the next two years, more equally disturbing advertisements appeared on the streets and in the daily newspapers. One showed army fatigues and a blood-stained T-shirt with a bullet hole and a headline reference to the conflict in Bosnia. Another showed two children: one white and angelic-looking, the second black with hair in the shape of satanic horns. A third showed a car in flames in the street after a terrorist attack. Perhaps the most moving and the most memorable showed an emaciated young man suffering from AIDS, lying on a bed, clearly close to death and being comforted by distraught members of his family.

Often when advertising comes under fire as breaching public taste, the fault is laid at the door of its advertising agency where, it is supposed, cynical and callow young creative people continually push beyond the boundaries of good taste simply to promote sales of their clients' products and earn arty awards.

In Benetton's case, such accusations could not be levelled because the company designed its own advertising, under its own creative director, Oliviero Toscani. The company's agency, J Walter Thomson, simply bought the advertisement hoardings and booked the space in magazines and newspapers.

Benetton is a privately-owned company, founded in 1965 and headquartered in Treviso, Italy, but with stores throughout Europe. It is headed by patriarch Luciano Benetton, who is a prominent Italian Senator. The man responsible for the controversial ads, Oliviero Toscani, has been a fashion photographer since the 1960s – a sort of Italian David Bailey. He is a close personal friend of the Benetton family and was the driving force behind the use of controversial and striking images in what the company claims is the ground-breaking use of advertising to make editorial statements.

Media explosions large and small were sparked off by the campaign, and thousands of column inches appeared, not merely in the advertising and marketing trade press, but in the national press where the images from Benetton's ads became a *cause célèbre*. Intense opposition was aroused by the campaign and many people announced that they were boycotting Benetton's shops as a result.

In Germany, the ads aroused such public anger that the shops were widely boycotted and German high street retailers actually sued Benetton for driving customers away and causing a loss of earnings. After due deliberation, the German courts rejected the claim as unfounded, but the fact that the case was brought at all is a clear sign that something had gone radically wrong.

When such controversial advertisements appear, it is not uncommon for the Advertising Standards Authority to get scores of complaints from the public. When the Benetton poster of the bloody baby appeared, the ASA received a record 800 objections from all over the country. The complaints were, says the Authority, that the ad was both 'extremely offensive and distressing'.

In its adjudication, the ASA said that, 'It was noted that before publication the advertisers, through their space-booking agency, had been advised by the Committee of Advertising Practice [a voluntary industry watchdog] not to run the advertisement as it was likely to provoke widespread offence. Media had been similarly advised. The Authority expressed its strong concern that the advertisers, their agency and the media had nonetheless elected, despite this advice, to proceed with the advertisement in a nationwide campaign featuring 48-sheet posters. In the Authority's view, such action displayed a conspicuous disregard for the sensitivities of the public and was a poor reflection on the advertising industry. The advertisers agreed to withdraw the poster.'[2]

The note of indignation was unmistakable. Not only had Benetton flouted good taste, it had even been warned in advance about the likely response to its ad precisely because of the outrage that greeted its previous ads.

Not everyone was against what Benetton had done, however. Tim Mellors, creative director of advertising agency GGT, argued cogently in the ad trade press in favour of the campaign. 'Surely,' he said, 'social issues like smoking, under-age drinking and the presentation of women as anorexic role models are fuelled by far more mendacious ads from other advertisers and their agents.

'I admire Benetton,' continued Mellors, 'because they are willing to stand up and be counted. They don't just have black, white and yellow kids in their ads, they have them serving in their shops.

'Sure you could question what a Kalashnikov rifle or an AIDS patient on his deathbed has to do with leggings and polo-necks. But perhaps what we should be questioning is whether the wonderful world of smiling families and dreamy interiors so many other advertisers still peddle isn't obscenely anachronistic in the Bosnian 90s.'

The creator of these controversial advertisements, Oliviero Toscani, was unrepentant. He told the *Sunday Times*, 'I suspect the English like animals more than human beings. My photograph of a baby with its umbilical cord was banned because they cried: "Shocking! Shocking! So bloody!" But if it had been a newborn puppy they would have loved it.

'People accuse me of exploiting with shocking images but, during the agony, consumption continues. We're all selling something. Those who use sex and violence to sell are a bunch of morons. They exploit human weakness to sell a product and I believe it's worse than what I do, which is showing what's going on in the world.'

We are not, of course, concerned here with the ethics or propriety of Benetton's advertising. That is an issue for the company and for the Advertising Standards Authority, when and if complaints are received from the public. The question for us here is: what does this advertising tell us about Benetton's corporate state of mind and how it sees us, its customers?

Most complainants to the ASA felt it was self-evident that neither Benetton nor the creative director who conceived the advertisements have as their *commercial* aim the improvement of humanity's lot or the raising of our consciousness. The individuals who run Benetton may well hold idealistic views on the future of mankind or they may not as the case may be. But in creating a commercial advertisement they can have only one aim, and that is to sell more jumpers. As Toscani says, 'We're all selling something.'

One unexpected consequence of this case is that advertisements such as Benetton's are making customers everywhere realise that some commercial organisations are not credible witnesses on their own behalf; that they cannot be trusted to tell the truth about anything except that which the law compels them to – such as the ingredients of their products – and that everything else they say is likely to be deliberately misleading and deceptive or at best a half-truth. Indeed, when it comes to communicating with their customers and prospective customers, some commercial organisations are without conscience or honour.

In one sense Tim Mellors is clearly right: Benetton is being more open and truthful with its advertising than the saccharine drivel of much TV advertising, like the puppy dogs used to make Andrex lavatory paper advertising acceptable in our living rooms or the famous actors paid to drool convincingly over cheap, frozen, supermarket meals. But from the standpoint of the corporate image, he is surely mistaken. For when Benetton starts to play with the truth as an issue, it is merely reminding us that Benetton's aim in advertising is not to enlarge our consciousness or enhance our appreciation of the truth: it is to sell us more leggings and polo-necks; and that its motives must inevitably be suspect.

Benetton embarked on a dangerous game with this advertising because it was playing corporate Russian roulette – staking its entire corporate image on a single message. If you liked the ads, you would like the company: but if you didn't like the ads, you would find the company and everything it appeared to stand for repulsive. In the event, a large number of people didn't like what they saw, and, if the reaction of many customers is anything to go by, Benetton will continue to pay the price of its madcap posturing for some time to come.

In terms of human psychology, Benetton was demanding to be heard and accepted purely on its own terms: like the teenager who demands to be loved and listened to despite his filthy appearance and his dreadful 'arty' paintings or his heavy metal guitar playing. It is tempting to fall back on that deadly phrase 'a cry for help'; except that one of Europe's wealthiest retailers does not need any help from us.

CHAPTER TEN

GO HOME, MICKEY MOUSE
How companies handicap themselves...*and how Disney came to Europe*

In order to survive in the world of cut-throat competition they inhabit, large corporations need certain key qualities: the ability to predict in advance which products and services will be successful and which will not; an unerring nose for a market-beating success; the ability to innovate; quick marketing reflexes and the ability to adapt rapidly to changing conditions.

The reality is that the number of large corporations who possess these desirable qualities can be counted on the fingers of one hand. In the real world, most organisations are unable to spot a winner even when it is handed to them on a plate; have no means of knowing whether a new product will be successful; have little or no ability to innovate; and are as quick and adaptable as a 100,000-ton oil tanker running at full speed ahead.

The extent to which large corporations are unable to recognise real talent and originality has been the stuff of show-business legend for decades. Classics include Metro-Goldwyn-Mayer's famous verdict on Fred Astaire's screen test: 'Can't act. Can't sing. Can dance a bit', and EMI's decision to turn down the opportunity to sign up a new singing quartet from Liverpool called The Beatles.

Matters are no easier in manufacturing industry or commerce and, to complicate them even further, it isn't always the 'best of breed' product that wins the trophy. In the early 1980s, three separate standards for video recording vied for dominance of the market: Sony's Betamax, the

Philips 2000 system, and VHS. Recording engineers were universally agreed that both Betamax and Philips produced far superior recording quality, yet it was VHS that won the battle, for purely marketing reasons – an outcome that few could have predicted.

But if large companies are so bad at recognising the winners of the future, where does innovation come from if not from the R & D laboratories of the big corporations? In the main it comes from the talented individuals who are outside the corporate system. It was not one of the great Hollywood studios, with their wealth and power, who inaugurated the era of the special-effects blockbuster movie, but a single talented individual, George Lucas, who made *Star Wars* in 1977 and founded the special effects studio, Industrial Light & Magic, which made possible most later blockbuster SFX films such as *Jurassic Park* and *Toy Story*.

A long list of major modern innovations comes not from within large corporations but from lone outsiders, usually working without recognition or support and often ignored or derided when they attempt to interest major manufacturers in their products. The list of outsiders includes: Philo Farnsworth and television; Whittle and the jet engine; Chester Carlson and xerography; Eckert and Mauchly and the commercial computer; Edwin Land and Polaroid photography; Christopher Cockerell and the hovercraft, and many more.

Even where the innovator belongs to a recognised institution, he or she is often a loner who achieves success by swimming against the currents of orthodoxy; like Alan Turing and the first British computers, or Eric Laithwaite and the magnetically levitated monorail train.

This reliance on innovation by heretics and outsiders is not a sad tale from a vanished past but is still very much with us today. Probably the most important chemical invention since the Second World War is that of a thin plastic coating that is able to withstand temperatures of 2,700 degrees Celsius. The invention does not come from the well-equipped laboratories of Britain's major chemical companies, but from the garden shed of a former women's hairdresser and amateur inventor, Maurice Ward.

Other examples confirm that even where innovations do come from within giant corporations, they are often critically dependent on the originality of a few individuals. In the pharmaceuticals industry, for example, the two greatest successes of recent years have been beta-blockers (now widely used in treating hypertension) and histamine-2 antagonists (effective against stomach ulcers), both of which came from the mind of one man, Dr Jim Black.

Some corporations spend billions but do not have even a Jim Black to show for it. In March 1992, the *Wall Street Journal* wrote: 'Despite spending of more than $13 billion...over the past ten years, DuPont's 5000 scientists and technologists were a technological black hole. They sucked money in, but, company officials concede, didn't turn out a single all-new blockbuster product or even many major innovations.' The *Journal* advised DuPont to 'restructure a bloated bureaucracy'.

But here even the respected *Journal* was missing the point, I believe. DuPont became big and famous in the 1940s and 1950s because it held the patents on nylon. But it wasn't a restructured or streamlined bureaucracy that enabled it to innovate such a blockbuster product, or even a highly-financed research facility. It was the mind of one exceptional man – Wallace Carothers – and a once-in-a-lifetime window of opportunity to discover a substitute for silk. Even $13 billion and 5000 scientists were no substitute for that fruitful opportunity or Carothers' originality.

But even if they do possess the rare ability to innovate, the central problem for most large organisations lies quite simply in their inability to say what the future will bring. When prediction proves difficult or impossible for them, as in the cases above, some companies unconsciously substitute self-deluding behaviour, which makes them feel as though they are able to predict the future successfully. A classic example of this behaviour is that of GOSPlan, the organisation (now thankfully disbanded) that was charged with the central planning of the economy of the former Soviet Union.

Occupying dozens of floors in a Moscow skyscraper, GOSPlan economists and planners were fed raw data, collected from the remotest corners of the Soviet Union, on production of food and raw materials and their consumption in industry and the home. Just like the raw materials entering the factories it studied, this raw information became more refined as it progressed up the GOSPlan building until, at the very top floor, the USSR's keenest economic brains converted the statistics into the next five year plan to which every citizen was obliged to conform. Central to GOSPlan's success in all this was the ability of its planners to predict accurately production and demand in the immediate future.

An example of the kind of thing that GOSPlan's efforts led to was the case of the Moscow launderette that was ordered by the plan to contribute two tons of scrap metal each year. If this scrap metal was not forthcoming, the launderette's managers would be personally liable to pay a substantial financial penalty. As a result, each year they were obliged to buy – sometimes even to steal – two tons of scrap steel in order to fulfil their commitment to the state plan.

The reason for the demand upon them was that some years earlier, they had unwisely decided to modernise the launderette, had installed modern washing machines and tumble-driers and – without realising the consequences of doing so – had scrapped the old machines. The all-powerful plan had logged this event and now demanded a comparable contribution each year. [1]

This kind of thing is so insane that one is inclined to think it could never happen outside of the planned economy of a totalitarian state. Yet the consequences of some product decisions taken in the freedom of the West have, if anything, been even more self-defeating.

Take, for example, the case of Thomas Midgley Junior, an acclaimed engineer and chemist who, in 1933, was appointed director of the Ethyl-Dow Chemical Company. Midgley had a dream of employing chemistry to improve the lot of his fellow men and women. In 1921, Midgley discovered tetraethyl lead and added it to petrol to improve the smooth running of car engines. In 1933, Midgley discovered the first of an important new class of organic gases called CFCs or Freons that were to become used the world over as refrigerants and as propellants for aerosols. In the 1940s, 1950s and 1960s, Midgley's Freon-powered aerosols were used to spread the pesticide DDT over billions of acres of farmland and countryside throughout the world. [2]

The consequences of Midgley's scientific discoveries and his company's products are not fully calculable but they include: depletion of the ozone layer with resulting increase in ultraviolet radiation and skin cancer; pollution of the Earth's atmosphere with dangerous levels of lead (levels that are continuing to increase despite legislation on car emission because the number of vehicles is increasing); the poisoning of countless endangered wild species of insects, birds and animals; and the promotion of super-resistant strains of dangerous pests like the malarial mosquito. The long-term effect of this pollution on the food-chain is incalculable, but more than one naturalist has speculated that it could include the extinction of all animal life on Earth.

Midgley's intentions were not destructive. On the contrary, he was a humanitarian, motivated by a desire to use science in the service of his fellows to enhance life. Unwittingly – and unforeseen by anyone else – his discoveries polluted our environment in an immensely destructive way that cannot be halted immediately, that will continue with increasing destructiveness for decades, and that will have consequences that, even with our increased knowledge, we still cannot accurately predict.

When companies are unable to predict the future, their usual course of action is to continue to do things as they have always done them, and to hope that what worked in the past will also work in the future.

How Disney Came to Europe

Whose is the most widely recognised face on earth? The answer is not the President of the United States nor Madonna nor Michael Jackson, but a geriatric cartoon rodent from Hollywood. Mickey Mouse's ears and grin are universally known to the extent that remote, illiterate tribespeople will point and smile excitedly at his cartoon image. In every country of the world, children and adults not only recognise Mickey instantly but also feel that they know him almost as a personal friend. Every few years, the same urban folklore rumour sweeps the globe that the studio is thinking of killing off Mickey Mouse, and the world is duly outraged at the mere thought of such a crime against such a well-loved friend.

What is perhaps oddest of all about this phenomenon is that the loveable mouse is nothing more than a brand image, owned by the Walt Disney studios, and traded commercially for profit. Mickey Mouse is as much a piece of corporate property as the waste-baskets at Paramount or the coat-hangers at MGM. Yet, paradoxically, we all feel as though we own a part of him in a way that we do not feel about, say, Ford cars or Colgate toothpaste.

There are quite a few brands that have this 'public ownership' feel to them: products that have become so well known that we unconsciously feel they are part of our lives, even though they are actually owned by someone else. In some cases the brand names have become part of our language and culture: Rolls-Royce, Hoover, Corn Flakes. As described earlier, Coca-Cola's attempts to tinker with the taste of Coke was seen as tantamount to tampering with Motherhood and Apple Pie.

This familiarity can be a priceless asset from a purely commercial point of view. But it is also a very dangerous asset. Imagine the likely effects on public opinion of putting a bullet into Mickey Mouse, or even allowing him to fool around with anyone other than Minnie, and you have some idea of the dangers. Quite simply, because we, the public, imagine that we own, or have a personal stake in these famous brands, we also tend to imagine that we should be consulted whenever any important decisions are taken involving them – and we tend to feel betrayed when we are not consulted or our feelings are ignored.

It was against this background that the Disney organisation planned to bring its immensely successful theme park idea to Europe. Yet it was in the full knowledge that what was at stake was nothing less than Mickey Mouse's reputation that the organisation plunged into the one of the most self-defeating marketing exercises of recent years.[3]

Disney planned to open Europe's first Disneyland early in 1992. The $4,400 million enterprise would cover a huge 5,000-acre site with six hotels and with plans for a second theme park. There would also be offices, apartments, shopping malls, golf courses and holiday homes.

The company predicted that 11 million Europeans would visit the theme park in the first year alone. Europeans already accounted for 2.7 million visits to Disneyland and Disneyworld in the US, so a forecast of 11 million visitors seemed reasonable. Indeed, in the US with its population of 250 million, there were 41 million visitors a year to Disney parks, so Europe's 370 million people ought to provide even more.

Not only are there more people in Europe, but they enjoy longer holidays than their American counterparts. French and German workers both get an average five weeks off a year compared with only two to three weeks in the US.

Like D-Day planners, Disney executives ordered copies of large-scale maps of every European country and demographic charts. Where should EuroDisney be sited, they wondered, as they gathered round the boardroom table and pored over the maps, chewing thoughtfully on their marker pens?

The maps became covered with felt-tip notations as some 200 European locations were examined one after another. There was the warmth of Spain; the wealth of Germany; the culture of Italy; the tradition and history of England: all countries that have much in common with American traditions and that welcome American culture. Instead, Disney chose to site its new park in the wettest, coldest part of France, a country that is notoriously intolerant of other nations and one with a particular hatred of American pop culture, which it regards as vulgar, cheap and tacky.

It is not merely with the benefit of hindsight that the decision is incomprehensible: it was equally incomprehensible at the time.

Three major $150 million amusement parks had opened in France between 1987 and 1991. By the time Disney was planning to start up, all three had flopped, with two in bankruptcy.

EuroDisney chairman Robert Fitzpatrick brushed these failed enterprises aside as having lacked Disney's flair and financial resources: 'We are spending 22 billion French francs before we open the door, while the other places spent 700 million. This means we can pay infinitely more attention to detail – to costumes, hotels, shops, trash baskets – to create a fantastic place. There's just too great a response to Disney for us to fail.'[4]

The French government was keen to attract Disney and allowed the company to buy up huge tracts of land at 1971 prices. It also provided

$750 million in loans at favourable rates of interest and spent hundreds of millions of public money on extending the Paris Metro and on building a new railway station for the high-speed train, making the site easily accessible from Paris.

But if the government was keen, many French people were less happy. Objectors organised demonstrations at EuroDisney's first shareholders meeting in Paris, pelting directors with eggs and displaying 'Mickey Mouse Go Home' signs for the benefit of TV cameras and press photographers.

French intellectuals and the French press were scathing about the plans, calling the idea of the park an American cultural abomination. The outcry was enough to cause French government officials to press Disney quietly for the theme park to be less obviously American in content and more European, with the result that Hollywood-style Swiss chalets and English villages complete with bobbies started to appear in the plans.

It was not merely in its strategic concepts that EuroDisney was deeply flawed but also in the design details that its chairman had hoped would be its key to triumph. The trash baskets were fine: it was in the basic eating and drinking and travel arrangements that the mistakes were made.

France, and its adjoining countries, are nations who universally drink wine with their meals. Disney declared EuroDisney to be non-alcoholic (though they have since reversed this rule). Europeans wish to sit down to eat. Disney provided fast food takeaways in line with American preferences for 'grazing on the hoof'.

Most Europeans travel to theme parks by coach. Even though this was made clear to Disney, it built rest room facilities for only 50 coach drivers. On peak days, 2,000 coaches were arriving from all over Europe, leaving their drivers with nowhere to shower, change or rest while waiting.

Even where they did conduct market research or listen to local advice, Disney still got it wrong. One Disney executive said that they were told Europeans did not eat breakfast, so they reduced the size of the restaurants (in a country famed for taking breakfast in restaurants). The consequence was that when the park opened they were trying to serve breakfast to 2,500 people in 350-seat restaurants.

All of this might have been no more than teething troubles had it not been for the fact that Disney's central predictions regarding its visitors were also catastrophically wrong.

Disney had assumed that demand for its products was insatiable and not price sensitive. Accordingly it had priced admission to the park at $42 – more expensive than the US parks. A night at one of Disney's best hotels would cost you $340; much the same as staying at a top Paris hotel, with the result that the hotels stayed half empty – the new rail and metro links were so efficient they enabled people to stay in Paris, 30 minutes away.

Food and drink was priced highly as well, with the result that canny French visitors simply brought packed lunches with them or ate when they got back to Paris.

The danger of overpricing quickly became obvious when people in Britain discovered that it was actually cheaper to fly to Disneyworld in Orlando, Florida, on one of the many bargain package holidays available – though even the most superficial research would have revealed this simple calculation.

Even worse for Disney executives was the discovery that whereas in America visitors stayed for four days on average, in Europe they stayed only a day or two at most. Typically, a family would visit the park on day one, spend only one night in a hotel, check out next morning, spending day two in the park before going home in the evening.

Unlike Florida and California, the weather in Northern France is often cold and wet with the result that the park was often sparsely populated. But despite that, EuroDisney met its projections in terms of numbers of visitors. An average of a million people a month visited EuroDisney in its first year.

The problem was, they didn't stay as long as expected, eat or drink as much as expected, or buy as much merchandise as expected, with the result that at the end of its first year, the company had made a loss of $921 million.

Under the deal it originally made with the European company, the Disney organisation back in the US would receive royalty fees only if the park broke even after servicing its large and growing debt to French banks. Disney chairman Michael Eisner threatened to pull out unless the European banks restructured the debt to give EuroDisney some breathing space and his company a prospect of recovering its investment. No one took the threat to pull out as anything other than a negotiating ploy, but it was a clear sign that Disney US was impatient with the failure of the European organisation to deliver.

Equally, Mickey Mouse was unlikely to take the advice of French intellectuals and go home, but he was not a happy rodent. He was cold and wet in a foreign country, with little prospect of making any money in the near future. And even his famous grin began to waver.

Happily, EuroDisney finally woke up to the special needs of the European market, changed its approach and its fortunes have been turned around – to such an extent that one of its former executives was later employed to attempt to salvage Britain's Millennium Dome project. But it was only when Disney stopped applying a formulaic way of doing things, and returned to its own innovative roots, that the company's fortunes changed for the better.

What is perhaps most ironic of all in Disney's example is that the organisation began its life by being highly innovative. The full-length cartoons like *Snow White*, devised by the young Walt Disney in the 1930s, were regarded as heretical by the established Hollywood studios, who predicted that audiences would not watch them. The theme park, invented by Disney, was also a 'first' for the entertainment industry. In each case, Disney the innovator fought for the cash and resources to make his vision a reality, against opposition from all those who saw only failure. Significantly, it was when the Disney organisation became wealthy and successful that it lost the plot and started to believe its own press releases about the future.

CHAPTER ELEVEN

NOT INVENTED HERE
How companies fail to innovate…*and how ICI couldn't stand the heat*

Of all the many ways in which organisations handicap themselves, the most self-defeating is a reluctance to believe that a single individual, working alone in what Americans evocatively call a 'skunk works', might make the major breakthrough that has eluded the teams of highly-qualified and highly-paid researchers that staff the company's well-appointed research and development laboratories.

This blindness to anything 'not invented here', and its accompanying belief that nothing of any real significance could be discovered by a lone outsider has cost many companies dear over the past few decades.

Radio Corporation of America is one of the world's largest and most powerful corporations. As well as being a major manufacturer of electronics and communications equipment, its claim to major status is its ownership of the National Broadcasting Corporation – NBC – one of the great US radio and television networks.

If you look into RCA's public relations brochures and its corporate history, you will find proud references to the company being 'first in the field' of television and drawing attention (quite rightly) to the pioneering achievement of the head of its research staff, Vladimir Zworykin, who developed the Iconoscope camera. What the brochures will not tell you is the real story of the invention of television, a story far more remarkable than any achievement of RCA, and of how RCA's powerful chief executive, David Sarnoff, was humiliated by an Idaho farm boy called Philo T Farnsworth.

In the early 1920s, a number of far-sighted researchers were starting to flirt with the idea of television. In 1922, Britain's John Logie Baird started his experiments with a part-electrical, part-mechanical system of low definition TV. The following year, in the United States, RCA chairman, David Sarnoff, predicted that 'every broadcast receiver for home use in the future will be equipped with a television adjunct by which the instrument will make it possible to see as well as hear what is going on in the broadcast station'. In RCA's laboratories, Vladimir Zworykin and his team were starting to try to crack the technical problems.

Unknown to these influential individuals – all of whose names are linked historically with the invention and development of television – a complete blueprint for a scanning electronic television system, including both cameras and receiving sets, had already been drawn in chalk on a schoolroom blackboard by the 15-year-old Philo Farnsworth, two years earlier in 1921.

Farnsworth's vision is even more extraordinary because he came from a poor farming family in Idaho, who could not afford to buy books for him. As a young boy he had discovered a pile of old popular science magazines, which fired his imagination and started his largely self-taught technical education.

When, at 15, he sketched his ideas for a television system on the blackboard, his chemistry teacher told him that he did not understand the invention but was so impressed that he encouraged the young boy to continue to develop his ideas and to try to make a working model.

Such development required finance, and Farnsworth's teacher helped him write letters to corporations large and small seeking capital to fund research. The big corporations to whom he wrote consigned his letters to the 'crackpot inventor' file, but one exceptionally far-sighted local businessman in Idaho agreed to put up some cash to keep the young Farnsworth busy in his garden shed – a remarkable act of confidence in a teenager.

The results exceeded anyone's expectations. In Los Angeles in September 1927, still aged only 21 years, Farnsworth gave the first public demonstration anywhere in the world of a practical working electronic television system. Telephone giant AT&T had demonstrated a rudimentary system five months before, but this was simply an exhibition piece with a high 'gee whizz' factor but limited practical use. Farnsworth, on the other hand, had anticipated and solved almost every problem connected with TV cameras, picture transmission and synchronisation, and the design of a home receiver that anyone could buy and use.

His undoubted lead over even the biggest laboratories enabled him to apply for a patent in 1927.

The patent application from an unknown 21-year-old hit the big corporations like a bombshell. David Sarnoff, impatiently awaiting results from his multi-million investment in television research, had anticipated possible rivalry from AT&T, but not from an Idaho farm boy. Furious, Sarnoff ordered his lawyers to contest the Farnsworth patent through to the highest courts.

Despite spending many thousands of dollars attempting to prove that his company, not Farnsworth, had invented television, Sarnoff was defeated and in August 1930, the 24-year-old young man was awarded his patent and a place in the history books as the inventor of television.

Vladimir Zworykin visited Farnsworth's laboratory in San Francisco to see the system for himself. Farnsworth's wife, Elma, recalled, 'When he saw the first television picture in Phil's lab, which was quite a clear picture, he said, "Beautiful, I wish I had invented it myself." '

The proud Sarnoff, who had so publicly promised RCA's customers a television in their homes, now had to instruct his lawyers to start the long and expensive process of trying to buy the Farnsworth patents.

The technology that Farnsworth had exploited so successfully to get a lead over even the largest corporations, and the area in which he proved to have such prodigious skill, was thermionic valves – or vacuum tubes – and their close relative, the cathode ray tube.

The first valve was invented by Britain's Ambrose Fleming in 1904 and made fully practical by American physicist Lee de Forest in 1906, only 15 years before the schoolboy sketched his drawing on the blackboard. The application of these vacuum tubes was still in its infancy. To make his television system work, Farnsworth had to develop all the important component parts, none of which was commercially available. This included such exotic items as image dissectors, pulse transmitters, synchronising oscillators, synchronous scanning image analysers and special cathode ray tubes. Farnsworth invented, designed and hand-built all of them himself. It was thus a largely practical skill that Farnsworth had mastered at his garden shed glass-blowing furnace, which gave him a vital edge over the scientists and technicians who had adopted a mainly theoretical approach to television.

Similar stories can be found even inside 'official' research. James Watson and Francis Crick were able to discover the structure of the DNA molecule largely because Watson – a self-confessed novice in the field of DNA – insisted on making physical models of the molecules they were working on. This practice, which Watson had imported from his native America, was frowned on by Oxford scientists of the 1950s who were accustomed to completing *The Times* crossword in their heads and felt that playing with toys was lowering the tone of the university.

Yet it was when playing around paper-clipping together cut-out paper models of the nucleotide bases – adenine, cytosine, guanine and thymine – that Watson first noticed the complementary shapes that resulted from combining them in pairs; one of the crucial insights that made the discovery of the DNA double helix possible.

Of course, many scientists and engineers today have a very different outlook from those of forty or seventy years ago, and using models of molecules is now standard practice. But large corporations are still putting letters from outsiders into their 'crackpot' files – and still getting it spectacularly wrong.

How ICI Couldn't Stand the Heat

With an annual turnover of more than £12 billion, Imperial Chemical Industries is Britain's fifth largest corporation and a world centre of excellence in chemistry research and development.

ICI has a long and illustrious history of innovations in basic chemical discoveries. Today its laboratories conduct encyclopaedic researches to try to discover new synthetic materials, new paints and coatings, new adhesives and a score of other uses for chemistry.

Yet what is probably the most important chemical discovery since the Second World War does not come from the well-equipped laboratories of Britain's major chemical companies, but from the garden shed of a former women's hairdresser and amateur inventor, Maurice Ward.

The holy grail of chemistry for fifty years or more has been a material that can be applied in a coating, like paint, and that will withstand intense heat. Such a product has such wide application in so many markets that it is guaranteed revenues of billions.

In April 1993, the defence magazine *Jane's International Defence Review* announced the discovery by a British amateur inventor, Maurice Ward, of a thin plastic coating able to withstand temperatures of 2,700 degrees Celsius. This remarkable material withstands temperatures an order of magnitude greater than that of ordinary paints or plastic coatings. It was considered news by a defence publication because the ability to withstand temperatures this high is enough to make tanks, ships and aircraft impervious to the heat of nuclear weapons at quite close ranges and is hence of great interest to the military. [1]

Most people found the reports incredible and the reaction of chemists and military experts alike was one of skeptical amusement. No known paint or plastic could resist temperatures anything like this without crackling and burning like paper. The smiles disappeared when Ward's invention was demonstrated on the BBC television programme *Tomorrow's World*.

Presenter Michael Rodd showed an ordinary chicken's egg that had been sprayed with an imperceptibly thin coating of Ward's new wonder plastic. Theatrically donning a welder's visor and fireproof gloves, he then calmly set about lighting an oxy-acetylene blow torch and playing the cutting flame directly onto the egg. [2]

After several minutes of this treatment, Rodd then picked up the egg and broke it into a bowl, showing that despite the temperature of thousands of degrees to which its outside had been subjected, the egg was still raw inside. The heat had not even penetrated an eggshell.

Inside ICI and other major chemical companies, questions began to be asked. Who on earth was the unknown man who had produced such an extraordinary material? What was its formula? How much did he want for it? And why hadn't it been found by professional R and D laboratories?

The inventor himself was a character straight from central casting. A somewhat reclusive and down-to-earth Lancashire man in his fifties, Maurice Ward has done a wide variety of jobs, and is without any scientific or other academic qualifications. He even spent a number of years doing manual work on the factory floor in ICI. More recently he has for some years run a ladies hairdressing salon in his native Blackburn.

Most of the women who visited his hairdressing salon also bought hair care products: shampoo, conditioner, hairspray and the like. Ward saw an opportunity to increase his income by selling his own range of hair products and set up a small factory where he began experimenting. By his own account, it was while simply mixing up the chemical constituents of such hair products that he stumbled across his wonder chemical.

Ward was at something of a loss to know what to do next. He realised his invention was worth billions and would need to be exploited by a major corporation, so he contacted ICI and offered them a demonstration. The executives he spoke to in ICI patiently explained to him that no material possesses the qualities he claimed and asked him to stop wasting their time.

The seriousness with which ICI today takes the invention can be gauged from the fact that the former head of research at the company has now joined Ward as technical director of the company he has formed to exploit the material.

Ward has called his material 'Starlite' and says that it contains 21 ingredients that can be mixed in a blender. He refuses to patent it, since that would mean disclosure of its formula. He has been conducting negotiations for some years with US government agencies including NASA, the Navy and the FAA (Federal Aviation Authority), and is reported to be close to a financial agreement.[3]

In the wake of the Maurice Ward affair, a red-faced ICI admitted it had rejected Ward's offer of his invention. To its credit, ICI conducted an internal audit of its laboratories and its research procedures in an attempt to determine how such an important basic chemical discovery could have eluded the might of ICI and yet have been so obvious to a garden shed inventor. What the company found was that all of its many patents and chemical discoveries were due mainly to the efforts of a tiny core of researchers and that far from being the most academically well-qualified, the innovative few were those with the least academic qualifications – in the case of the most prolific inventor, no qualifications at all. The innovators were those who had not been taught to think.

Whether ICI and other large organisations will be able to learn from their mistake over Maurice Ward's plastic remains to be seen. But it seems likely that letters from 'crackpot inventors' will at least be scrutinised more carefully in future.

Failure to innovate, as in the case of ICI here, or that of DuPont, highlighted by the *Wall Street Journal*, seems to be associated with the age and size of the organisation, rather like arthritis. The older and fatter the company, the less it likes surprises.

For many institutions a century ago, this natural tendency to resist change was a benefit. Customers of the Banks, White Star Lines, the Great Western Railway or Selfridges, wanted the reassurance of conservatism and continuity – hence the solid architecture and the top hats. For most organisations in the twenty-first century, such solidity is nothing more than a hardening of the arteries, and is likely to prove just as fatal.

CHAPTER TWELVE

THEY WOULD SAY THAT, WOULDN'T THEY?
How to predict companies' behaviour...*and how BNFL told a glowing tale*

One way to predict a company's future behaviour is to look at its past record. Of course, extrapolation is a risky business. The fact that a company has behaved well towards customers in the past is no guarantee that it won't go off the rails in future; and the fact that a particular organisation is an old lag who has been caught out in lies more times than anyone can remember is no guarantee that it might not make a supreme effort to do the decent thing this time.

But in general, the rule with organisations of all kinds, as with people, is that what you see is what you get, and past behaviour is as good a starting point as any other.

But if predicting future behaviour is difficult, accounting for present behaviour is just as hard. Asking why organisations do the things they do is generally a fruitless question. You might think that since many corporations' commercial objectives are identical and their products or services very similar, that their structure and methods would also be similar. In fact, I have never found two companies that were exactly like each other in their methods or approach, even if they are in the same business.

Take the large US software houses, for example; companies like Oracle, Microsoft, Borland, and Sybase. They sell very similar sorts of products, to the same customers, in competition for the same budgets. Senior staff move between companies as easily and as often as football stars transfer between teams and it is difficult nowadays to find a senior executive in one company who has not already worked for several of the others. Yet the differences in company culture and methods can be as great as between a motor manufacturer and a fish and chip shop.

On the first occasion I visited the headquarters of Oracle, the biggest database vendor, in 1989, the company's marketing communications manager astounded me by telling me that his department took up an entire floor of the building and had more than 50 staff. In many large companies, five PR staff would be considered too many. What on earth did this army of PR people do all day, I wondered? Surely there aren't that many business editors in Britain for them to speak to? I later discovered that his company pursued the policy of attending every single exhibition that took place in Britain that had even the remotest connection to his company's main product and that it was the logistics of attending several exhibitions every week all over the country that took up so much time and effort.

Since Oracle at that time was selling around $1 billion worth of its database worldwide every year, its marketing communications policies seemed to be very effective, yet as far as I know its approach was unique – indeed many of its competitors shunned exhibitions as a waste of time.

Probably the only answer that can be given to the question: why do organisations do the things they do? is simply that they are done because they are possible. Why did the German army devote immense resources to designing and building the V2 rocket, an uneconomic and inefficient weapon of war? Because it was technically feasible. To an artillery man, the rocket appeared to be the ultimate cannon shell. Why did the Pentagon build an atomic bomb? For similar reasons. An interesting example of this phenomenon, also from the Second World War, concerns British Intelligence's famous coup, the decryption of German Enigma signals traffic.

Since the publication of Frederick Winterbotham's *The Ultra Secret* in 1974, few people remain unaware of the key part played in the last war by Ultra intelligence – the top secret decoding of German military coded messages from Enigma machines by MI6 at Bletchley Park. What is not well known is why the secret was kept so well and so long after the war.[1]

117

The reason is that the Foreign Office and Secret Intelligence Service found reading secret German messages during the war so informative and enjoyable, they thought they would like to carry on reading other people's mail after the war. They accordingly set up a 'cover' factory to make Enigma type machines and sell them to corporations and governments around the world, knowing perfectly well that only Britain possessed the ability to read Enigma traffic.

Throughout the 1950s and 1960s, governments friendly and unfriendly bought Enigma machines and thus provided Whitehall with unrivalled inside information about their intentions. By the mid-1970s, computers had taken over the role of old-fashioned electromechanical cypher machines and the ruse had no more life left in it. Winterbotham (who had run the Ultra organisation during the war) was thus given permission to disclose the secret in order that the Secret Intelligence Service could gain a little PR kudos from the wartime intelligence triumph.[2]

The key point in all this is the way MI6 continued to use the Ultra decrypting machinery for spying on friends and enemies alike after the war – not simply because it was advantageous, but because, for a time, it was *possible*.

For much the same reason, double-glazing companies sell replacement windows; airlines transport tourists; office equipment makers sell photocopiers. When electric road propulsion is a reality, Ever Ready and Exide will rent batteries at roadside stations, not because they want to, or merely because of its profit potential, but because it will be possible, and hence a natural thing for them to do. Perhaps it is more accurate to say that it will be easy for them to gain the approval of their peers and the community for their activities.

If a company is engaged in selling products and services of this sort that are approved of by the majority of people in the community, then its 'story' and behaviour are likely to be easily predictable. But in some cases, companies are trapped by the very nature of their product. Walter Scott warned, 'O what a tangled web we weave, when first we practise to deceive.' As we saw in the case of the asbestos companies some companies become trapped in a tangled web of their own deceit and, because they are unable to escape, must maintain the lies that are built into the very core of their businesses.

The most obvious example of this kind that springs to mind is British Nuclear Fuels (BNFL) who have no feasible alternative than to maintain that nuclear energy is an economical way to generate power, with no harmful side-effects on health, even when everyone else in Britain, including the government, has given up nuclear energy as a lost cause and no further nuclear power stations are to be built.[3]

To announce publicly that all nuclear power stations are uneconomic, and that many nuclear workers and their children have contracted cancers from radiation from nuclear installations, would spell the end of their industry and open the floodgates to hundreds of claims for compensation running into billions of pounds.

Cornered even more tightly, if that is possible, are the tobacco companies. No rational person doubts any longer that there is the clearest possible relationship between smoking and lung cancer – indeed lung cancer as a primary site of the disease is practically unknown outside of smokers. Yet the tobacco manufacturers have no alternative but to continue gamely to insist that there is no actual proven link between the two and so there is, strictly speaking, no *conclusive* evidence that smoking is harmful.

It is hardly surprising that the cigarette companies should resist us making this link, but just in case anyone is in any doubt as to how badly their sales can be affected by it, there is the recent case of South Africa. In November 1995, the South African government decided to adopt statutory health warnings on cigarette packs.

There was no pussyfooting around with 'maybe' and 'sometimes' as there was in the early days of pack warnings in Britain. The South Africans got straight to the point with warnings such as: 'The More You Smoke, The Sooner You'll Die' and 'Danger: Smoking Can Kill You.'

This blunt speaking outraged South African farm workers so much that they began forming groups to shout protests outside tobacconists' shops. According to Johannesburg's *Business Day* magazine, protesters shouted such slogans as, 'Give us non-cancer packs...we want non-cancer packs now!'

According to the magazine, 'The irate farm workers are demanding the return of the unmarked packs that they used to be able to buy before the health warnings were added, because they think those weren't lethal.' Tobacconists, said *Business Day*, report that these workers absolutely refuse to buy the new packs.

Interestingly it was in connection with a study of beliefs regarding smoking and lung cancer that the concept of cognitive dissonance – roughly speaking, believing what you want to believe, like the irate farm workers – was first brought to public attention.

Leon Festinger and his colleagues at Stanford University coined the idea of cognitive dissonance – that we all strive to keep a sense of consistency between the things that we think we know and that we resist any new information that causes dissonance between our beliefs, or we strive to reduce that dissonance. [4]

One of the first studies on which Festinger based his theory of cognitive dissonance was a survey carried out in Minnesota in which people were asked: 'Do you think the relationship between cigarette smoking and lung cancer is proven or not proven?' The poll showed that the attitude of smokers and non-smokers to this question differed sharply. Among non-smokers, 29 per cent thought the link was proved and 55 per cent thought it not proved. Those who smoked heavily held very different views. Only 7 per cent of heavy smokers thought the link proved and a whopping 86 per cent thought it not proved.

The important question here is not the scientific question of who is right and who is wrong, but why smokers should hold such a strongly different belief from non-smokers. The answer that Festinger gives is that the smokers are acting to reduce their level of cognitive dissonance by denying the link – despite considerable medical evidence. Knowing they smoke and accepting the medical evidence would create a distressing inconsistency in their beliefs. The simplest way to reduce that distress is to deny the new information.

Seen from this standpoint, it is not simply a case of tobacco companies lying their heads off, so much as they and their customers attempting to reduce their mental discomfort to a minimum. For the seminal example of cognitive dissonance in action, though, nothing can come even close to the nuclear industry.

How BNFL Told a Glowing Tale

The centre of nuclear operations in Britain is the site named after the rural Cumbrian district of Sellafield. At least, it is known as Sellafield today, because in 1983 British Nuclear Fuels Limited, who operate the site, changed its name from Windscale: a name that, like the radioactive fuel rods in reactors sited there, had accumulated an unbearable burden of poison that had to be buried deep, to give the site a fresh start.[5]

BNFL must have hoped that a change of name might accomplish what thirty years of concerted public relations had conspicuously failed to do and change the public perception associated with the Windscale name: the perception that Windscale is a dangerous place.

The Calder Hall nuclear power station – the world's first commercial station – was opened at Windscale by a young Queen Elizabeth in October 1956; a proud symbol of Britain's leadership in nuclear engineering. Four years earlier, Britain's first nuclear reactors had begun quietly operating at Windscale with no public announcement or royal ceremony. These reactors were not designed to generate electricity but were simply piles for the transformation of enriched uranium into plutonium, for use in Britain's atomic weapons.

When the young Queen pressed the button that started atomically-generated power flowing to the national grid, few doubts were heard about the safety of these new stations. The Campaign for Nuclear Disarmament would not be founded until 1958. Only a small group of scientists, engineers and civil servants had any inkling that the new technology might not be safe, let alone that it could lead to disaster.

Exactly one year after the Queen officially opened Calder Hall, in October 1957, the disaster happened. The number one reactor pile at Windscale caught fire and burned uncontrollably for two days, causing a meltdown of its nuclear fuel and spreading more than five tons of radioactive fallout over Britain.

You don't have to be a nuclear physicist to see what can go wrong with a reactor pile of the Windscale type. The control rods are withdrawn until the uranium fuel rods go 'critical' and heat up, heating up also the graphite blocks that surround them. If the process should run away, out of control, then the uranium fuel rods and the graphite blocks will overheat and eventually catch fire. When the temperature gets high enough, the uranium fuel will melt and start to burn down through the core – the notorious 'China Syndrome'. If the temperature continues to rise still further, the uranium and other materials will eventually vaporise and disappear up the chimney into the atmosphere to fall on the surrounding countryside, animals, towns and people.

Given that this is the sole emergency the nuclear scientists and engineers have to fear and to plan for, you might imagine that they would have put in place measures specifically to prevent it. In fact, there were no such measures at Windscale. In the words of the man responsible for the design of the nuclear piles, Sir Christopher Hinton, they are 'monuments to our initial ignorance'.[6]

The design of Windscale incorporated a number of fans to blow air across the pile to keep its temperature down. Apart from inserting the control rods to damp down the nuclear chain reaction in the core, these cold air blowers were the *only* method provided to cool down the reactor if it overheated. Of course, if it caught fire, then the blowers would not cool down the pile but, on the contrary, would fan the flames, increasing the intensity of the fire. Thus, when the core temperature got dangerously hot, the blowers would have to be switched *off* rather than *on* in order to prevent a fire and there would no longer be any means available of cooling the pile.

If air could not be used to cool the reactor, what about water?

When Windscale was being designed, the scientists responsible believed that it would not be possible to put out a reactor fire by pouring water on it. Water would, they believed, merely make matters worse and should be kept as far away from the reactor pile as possible. Pouring water onto burning graphite might cause an explosive mixture of carbon monoxide, hydrogen and air. They also believed that pouring water over a highly radioactive core would irrevocably contaminate the rest of the structure and make it useless for future production. Thus the decision was deliberately taken not to provide fire hydrants in the pile buildings.

Even with all these obvious points of danger, the Windscale reactor piles might not have been subject to a disastrous accident if the operating staff were able to control the core temperature confidently at all times. However, it turned out they were not able to do this because merely operating the pile on a day-to-day basis caused a dangerous instability to build up in the graphite blocks. As these blocks were subjected to daily irradiation, the atoms in their crystal structure were displaced. Each time the pile was run, the graphite heated up and the stored energy it contained – predicted by physicist Eugene Wigner and hence known as Wigner energy – was released as the atoms returned to their natural positions.

It was in attempting to get rid of this unwanted Wigner energy, by allowing the pile to heat up in a controlled way, that the operating staff lost control of the pile and it caught fire. The exact starting point of the Windscale meltdown will never be known for certain. It might have been a pocket of excessively great Wigner energy. It might have been a microscopically small hole in one of the thousands of canisters that contained the uranium fuel rods, causing the uranium to oxidise on contact with the air.

Overall, it is difficult to imagine a design that could have been more dangerous. This judgement is not merely made today with the wisdom of hindsight: it was made at the time by some of those who saw the design taking shape. In 1949, Dr Edward Teller, the 'father of the hydrogen bomb', visited Windscale under construction. He warned that 'the most likely cause of a serious reactor accident, which could affect a very wide area, was the energy stored in irradiated graphite, especially if a fuel rod caught fire'.[7]

Because Teller's warning was ignored, or unknown to the designers, Windscale was completely unequipped to deal with a fire and meltdown when the number one pile caught alight in October 1957. Finding that they were compelled to switch off the cooling fans and had no other safety measures available, the Windscale operations staff were forced to improvise. They put on protective clothing and masks, grabbed scaffolding poles from the building site at Calder Hall, which was still partly under construction, and began a heroic effort standing at the charging face of the pile trying to push the burning fuel rods manually through the pile and out the back into a cooling pond. As they withdrew the scaffolding poles from the reactor core, the ends glowed red hot. By this means they created a fire-break around the reactor core, which stopped the fire spreading still further, but they were unable to dislodge the crucial burning fuel rods in the core because they had become distorted by the intense heat and jammed.

The Windscale fire and meltdown began shortly after midnight on Wednesday 9 October and burned all day Thursday. By Friday morning, things had become desperate. There was a slight possibility that if the fire-fighters had had access to massive quantities of some inert gas such as argon or carbon dioxide, they might have been able to blanket the fire, but they had no such materials available in quantities that would make any difference. Early on Friday morning, the engineers fighting the fire decided that desperate measures were called for. They took fire hoses from the site fire engine, tied them to scaffolding poles, thrust them into the reactor pile just above the fire and prepared to pour water on it in a last attempt to regain control.

There seemed a serious risk that this might cause an explosion, which would shower the surrounding countryside with radioactive debris. But if something wasn't done the whole core would melt, then vaporise, and go up the chimney anyway. The assistant works director, Tom Tuohy, courageously remained behind in the reactor building and gave the order to turn on the water, first at low pressure. Tuohy peered into the inspection holes, saw the glow diminish and called for the flow to be increased. Through the inspection hatch he saw the flames flicker and begin to die down. Thousands of gallons of water were poured onto the reactor and by noon the next day, the fire was out.

When the pile was cold, engineers began to evaluate what had happened. Before the fire, the pile had contained 180 tonnes of enriched uranium and nuclear products such as plutonium and polonium. The engineers estimated that about 17 tons of uranium had melted and burned through the core, and a further *five tons* had vaporised and gone up the chimney. From Windscale, these radioactive particles were carried by winds all over Northern Britain and beyond. On the way they contaminated the milk of thousands of cattle, and much else.

The prime minister, Harold Macmillan, ordered that the seriousness of the meltdown must not be made public knowledge and hence a series of anodyne press releases were issued by the Atomic Energy Authority, BNFL's precursor organisation as operators of Windscale. Ultimately a White Paper neutered of the true facts was published. It was at this time that many of today's stock euphemisms of the nuclear industry were coined, and first passed off on an unsuspecting press and public.

For example, the meltdown and loss of five tonnes of radioactive fuel, including an unspecified amount of weapons grade plutonium (the most toxic substance on earth) up Windscale's chimney and over Britain, was referred to as an 'incident', and even as a 'mishap'.

The main concern of the press and public was, of course, the health implications of the disaster. Soon after the fire had started, health physicists from Windscale began to monitor the surrounding area for radiation. Monitoring vans drove several miles around the plant in all directions for two days, continuously sampling and monitoring soil, vegetation, grass, milk and various foods. The physicists decided that there was no health hazard in the area from breathing in contaminated particles and that the only risk was from radioactive materials getting into the human food-chain. The worst contamination, they believed, was of milk by the short-lived radioactive isotope, iodine-131.

The guidelines on which health physicists worked in 1957 were the recommendations of the International Commission on Radiological Protection (ICRP). The Commission had made recommendations regarding the limits for lifetime exposure of radiation workers but it had not yet addressed the question of a once-in-a-lifetime emergency for the general population. Also its figures were based on the model of a standard adult, but not for a standard child or baby.

On the figures then available, and calculations quickly improvised, it was decided that it was safer to destroy all milk in an 80 square mile area around the site. Three days after the fire, the area was extended to 200 square miles, although children in the additional 120 square miles

125

around the plant had been drinking milk since the fire started. The same day as the toddlers were belatedly deprived of their school milk, a meeting of radiation experts took place in London. It was chaired by Sir Harold Himsworth, secretary of the Medical Research Council and chairman of the MRC committee on radiation hazards.

The committee unanimously agreed that 'the emergency actions, in so far as they concerned the hazard to man, were both well-conceived and adequate and that their rapid and efficient implementation reflected great credit on all concerned'. [8]

The committee also agreed that the accident should be regarded as a single 'incident', that no fallout after 12 October need be considered, and that the danger to the population from external radiation was negligible. The hazard to humans arose solely from radioisotopes entering the food-chain, but only liquid milk was of concern and meat, eggs and vegetables could be safely ignored, said the committee.

On the basis of these opinions, the Government White Paper of 1957 said confidently that it was 'in the highest degree unlikely that any harm [had] been done to anybody, whether a worker in the Windscale plant or a member of the general public'.

At first, press coverage of the meltdown was neutral – even favourable to the nuclear authorities: a reflection of the respect that the press had for science in the 1950s, and of the media's expectation that it would be told the truth by the government and Windscale's operators. Even *New Scientist* swallowed the party line and wrote, 'The accident...which resulted in radioactive iodine being released in small quantities over part of the Lake District caused much alarm. It could easily have resulted in opposition to the atomic power programme on which the country has embarked. But the official Windscale Report offers so frank and satisfying an explanation that the public is enabled to view the happenings of 10 October in proper perspective.'[9]

Two things happened in subsequent years to alter this complacent perspective. First it was realised that the radiological protection guidelines were not rigorous enough: people can be harmed by very small doses of radiation over longer periods of time. Second, it eventually dawned on people that the claim that five tons of radioactive particles could be scattered from the air over a large area of Britain without anyone breathing them in was fundamentally incredible.

The 'zero health hazard' claims of radiation experts in 1957 were gradually eroded in successive evaluations, culminating in the study of Peter Taylor of the Political Ecology Research Group in Oxford, in 1981. Taylor considered the probable effects of inhalation (previously ignored) and also looked at the effects of some dangerously long-lived radioactive elements such as polonium-210 (also previously ignored). He found that the radiation exposure received by the UK population because of the Windscale fire could result in between 10 and 20 cancer deaths, occurring over several decades. The number of thyroid cancer cases might be 250 of which 10 might be fatal.

These estimates were based on then currently accepted ICRP risk factors. However, many scientists then and now thought these risk factors too low. If, Taylor said, the ICRP risk factors were higher, and if thyroid cancer mortality was ten per cent, rather than five per cent, then the upper limit of cancer deaths caused by Windscale could be nearer *280 people* over several decades.

So, the bottom line was that Windscale's 'no health hazard' statement of 1957 had become up to 280 cancer deaths and hundreds more non-fatal cases by the time the full facts were beginning to trickle out twenty-five years later.[10]

Accidents have continued to happen at Windscale, sometimes serious ones. In 1974 there was a major accident when a serious fire, explosion and blowback put the first oxide reprocessing plant out of action. Today, there are on average ten accidents or, as BNFL prefers to call them, 'incidents', a year at Windscale. The site also continuously discharges small amounts of radioactive elements, including toxic materials such as plutonium, into the sea, claiming this is safe.

As the true facts about Windscale began to emerge, the people of Cumbria became more and more concerned about the safety of the site in their midst. In the coastal village of Seascale, two miles from Windscale, is a small community of some 2,000 people who provided many of the workers who built the Windscale plant and who later provided its workforce.

In 1983, a documentary film by Yorkshire TV, 'Windscale – the Nuclear Laundry' – revealed the alarming fact that there was an unusual cluster of leukaemia victims in Seascale. The Government ordered an independent enquiry, chaired by Sir Douglas Black, which found that there was indeed an increased incidence of leukaemia in people under 25 living in the area.

A series of medical studies were begun, principally under the direction of the late Professor Martin Gardner, an eminent medical statistician. His team discovered that young people living in Seascale were *ten times* more likely to develop leukaemia than the national average and *three times* more likely to develop other cancers. After a further study lasting six years, Gardner reached the conclusion that statistically, it was the father's exposure to radiation before his child was conceived that increased the chances of the child having leukaemia.

In PR terms, BNFL now found itself in exactly the same corner as the tobacco manufacturers. There was clear-cut evidence of a correlation between Windscale and leukaemia just as there was between cigarette smoking and lung cancer. But because no one could provide conclusive scientific evidence of a mechanism, it was possible for BNFL to continue to deny the existence of a proven *causal* link. Even when the cowboy who appeared in the famous Marlboro advertisements died of lung cancer, it was still technically possible for Philip Morris to insist that there was no proven link. And, no matter how many children died of leukaemia in Seascale, it was still possible for BNFL to insist that there was no proven connection with nuclear installations.

BNFL did, however, take action following the television film on leukaemia and Seascale's children: it quietly dropped the Windscale name and began to refer always to the site as Sellafield.

Professor Gardner continued to develop his theory, known as Paternal Preconception Irradiation or PPI, and the prestigious *British Medical Journal* published a paper on the subject in 1990. The medical community was set buzzing by the publication and the people of Seascale were naturally alarmed. Some scientists welcomed Gardner's concept of PPI while others challenged it.

Although Gardner has since died, research continues into PPI and possible alternative radiation-linked causes.

A number of parents were already planning to sue BNFL for damages over cancers contracted near Windscale and the publication of Gardner's findings gave them the ammunition they needed. Their solicitor, Martyn Day, chose two representative cases with which to fight and went into court backed by the evidence of the Gardner Report.

The cases contested were those of Elizabeth Reay, a 73-year-old, whose baby daughter, Dorothy, had died of leukaemia some 32 years earlier; and Vivien Hope, a 29-year-old, who developed non-Hodgkin lymphoma in 1988 and who was partly disabled as a result. In both cases, the women's fathers had been exposed to high doses of radiation at the Windscale site and it was this, said the claimants, which predisposed their children to develop cancer. The case thus turned on Gardner's PPI theory.

At the High Court in London, in October 1993, Mr Justice French found for the defendant, BNFL. The court decided that because of the absence of any supporting evidence, then on the balance of probabilities, PPI was not to blame for their cancers. In May 1994, the same judge dismissed similar claims from eight other families, but said the families could bring fresh proceedings if future scientific research suggested a causal link between nuclear installations and childhood cancer.

In a now familiar pattern, BNFL's public relations department transformed the finding of 'absence of evidence' for a cause into the one-word headline 'CLEARED' in the company newspaper. BNFL's annual report also claimed that the court had 'cleared BNFL of the allegations that radiation from Sellafield had caused leukaemia in children'.

So far, the further evidence regarding childhood cancer that the court spoke of has not been found. Yet, in 1992, the National Radiological Protection Board, which advises the Government on safety limits, carried out a study that showed for the first time a significant connection between the incidence of leukaemia deaths amongst workers at Sellafield and their exposure to relatively low doses of radiation over a long period of time.

The Board's study indicated that the risk presented by radiation in causing fatal leukaemia and other cancers is twice as great as previously thought. And it reached this conclusion after studying the records of some 95,000 people employed in the nuclear industry since 1945. Thus, while BNFL's PR department had been maintaining that the nuclear industry had a good safety record over the decades, radiation had been quietly killing twice as many people as anyone knew about.

But while the conclusive evidence of a causal link still eludes medical scientists, some new evidence having an important bearing on BNFL's attitudes has emerged.

The story that BNFL has tried to sell to the press is that the majority of local people accept the Sellafield site because they have a more detailed knowledge of the safety arrangements and of what really goes on inside what must necessarily be a closed and secretive site.

Much doubt has been cast on claims of this sort by a study conducted in 1994 by researchers from the Centre for the Study of Environmental Change at Lancaster University. The Lancaster team reported: 'Whilst the currently dominant economic role of BNFL at Sellafield has brought certain benefits to the area – namely large numbers of jobs and sponsorship for local activities – the industry's very dominance has led to something of a "dependency syndrome" in much of the local population. This in turn manifests itself for many local people in the "burying" of a range of personal ambivalences and anxieties about Sellafield, its operations and its implications.'

The report concludes: 'There is extensive local ignorance about the operations and processes used at Sellafield. Far from it being the case, as is sometimes claimed, that local acceptance of the industry rests on a greater than average understanding of nuclear power and its implications, such acceptance rests on a fatalistic acceptance of the dominant local economic and employment role of Sellafield, with the accompanying risks, in the absence of any realistic alternatives for the area... There is considerable local resentment at the perceived withholding of information about leaks and other pollution incidents at Sellafield when they occur. Even though such episodes represent genuine dilemmas for the industry, they are helping to intensify continuing patterns of mistrust of BNFL, fed by past controversies... The industry tends continually to undermine its credibility with local people by its insistence on giving the impression of comprehensive certainty or control. There would be benefits from a more trusting and less "anxious" approach to the public.'

Rather than adopting a 'more trusting and less anxious approach', BNFL has instead adopted a Disneyland approach to its PR problems. It has opened a multi-million pound 'Sellafield Visitors Centre', which gives a glimpse into the mind of the company. Visitors, especially children and school parties, can enter 'The World of BNFL', have fun with a friendly Mighty Atom character who comes to life, and 'experience the sensation of being in the heart of a reactor as nuclear fission releases incredible energy' – a phrase that to some ears will be uncomfortably reminiscent of October 1957, when people were able to experience the real thing at Windscale.

BNFL continues to insist that, 'Our record, for the safety of our workforce, compares favourably with similar industries.' The company also says that, 'The development of an effective safety culture has been crucial to achieving and maintaining the high safety standards the Company sets itself.'[11]

After the meltdown of 1957, the Windscale piles were switched off and the doors closed on them: their radioactive carcasses left until someone could work out what to do with them. They are still there forty years later, though a start has been made on dismantling the chimney-stacks.

In its current Company Profile, BNFL has even managed to turn Windscale's greatest disaster so far into a little useful PR copy. The company has, it says, 'unique experience of decontaminating redundant nuclear plant' adding, without a trace of irony, 'This is a growth area of business...' This cheerful admission is supported by a full-page picture of two BNFL decommissioning engineers, overseeing operations as they stand on top of the Windscale pile chimneys, dominating the beautiful Cumbrian landscape over which they spread so many tons of deadly radioactivity, in such secrecy, and all for nothing.

CHAPTER THIRTEEN

PUT NOT YOUR TRUST IN PRINCES

How corporations live in the past...*and how Perrier lost its mystique*

They each had their principality: their dynastic house; their majestic standard, its emblem easily recognisable at a glance in the field and worn by their many servants. Their immense wealth accrued from the tributes paid to them by their loyal subjects. They engaged in constant manoeuvring and posturing with other such princedoms, threatening warlike noises when necessary, but achieving their territorial ends by diplomacy whenever possible. Their merchant venturers carved up the world between them, allowing them to accumulate commercial wealth and power both at home and abroad.

This might be a description of mediaeval European princes and their competing states. It is, in fact, a description of modern multinational corporations.

When today's market researchers are seeking some inspiration or guidance on the likely shape of things to come, they usually look forward to the most highly developed markets they can find. If they want to know what will be happening in information technology, or in consumer goods, or in home entertainment in Britain in two years' time, they can visit the metropolitan United States or Japan and get a glimpse of the future at first hand.

When it comes to the difficult business of foreseeing the future of large corporations, things are not quite so simple. Shell, Ford, McDonald's, ICI and the rest, all operate on a global scale already, exporting their corporate culture wherever their sales and distribution operations set foot. There is no difference between a Big Mac or a litre of fuel whether it is bought in London, Los Angeles or Lusaka.

But despite the homogeneity of corporate culture today, there is somewhere we *can* go to get some clues to the likely future behaviour of large organisations: that foreign country which, according to L P Hartley, is so distinct because they do things differently there – the past.

It is no accident that multinational corporations closely resemble mediaeval princedoms. Both institutions have evolved out of the same necessities, for the same essential reasons and with the same objectives. The main difference is that five hundred years ago, such enterprises were the prerogative of the privileged few by virtue of birth and ambition, while today they are the prerogative of the privileged few by virtue of education, ability and ambition.

Niccolo Machiavelli, or any other intelligent, educated counsellor to a mediaeval prince would recognise at once the duties and daily concerns of his twentieth-century counterpart: the senior executive of a multinational corporation.

Of course, many things are different today compared with the 1500s. It is no longer considered acceptable to chop off your competitor's head with a broadsword – or, indeed, the head of an inconvenient royal wife. But what is remarkable are not the differences that can be found but the similarities.

European princes had as their main objectives the maintenance of their territories; the perpetuation of their house through marriage; and the expansion of their revenues through tribute, trade and (if necessary) war. At the same time, it was essential for princes to win and keep the loyalty and love of their people through generous and public-spirited deeds; to be seen always to act in a strictly legal and civilised way, dealing fairly with everyone, and to demonstrate clear, bold leadership.

These two sets of objectives – the business objectives and the public relations objectives – are bound to conflict with each other much of the time. Hence the art of the mediaeval prince was the art of Machiavelli –

133

that of appearing publicly to honour the spirit of fair play, while privately behaving as unscrupulously as necessary.

It is both the similarity of the two sets of objectives, and the similarity of the core contradiction, that makes mediaeval princedoms comparable with today's corporations. What Henry VIII or Cesare Borgia did and got away with yesterday, Shell and IBM are likely to do and get away with today: they are acting from the same motives, and within the same limitations, to achieve the same ends.

So exactly what pressures were mediaeval princes subject to? What solutions did they evolve to the problems they faced? And how are those solutions of service in understanding corporations today?

One outstanding characteristic of mediaeval monarchs is that they were able to command the most dedication and loyalty from their subjects when they faced their greatest challenges: yet their unwillingness to acknowledge or reward almost all those who helped them surmount those challenges was fathomless.

The greatest external challenge faced by Queen Elizabeth I during her long reign was the Spanish Armada. Thousands of England's fighting men faced the Spanish fleet in the Channel in 1588 and it was thanks to the courage, patriotism and fighting skill of her seamen, that Elizabeth kept her throne. Their reward from their sovereign once the armada was defeated was to be kept aboard their vessels at anchor, forgotten, their clothes in rags, without food, dying from starvation and disease, until the conscience of the nation was pricked and money was raised for their relief by public subscription.

Elizabeth was not an ungenerous woman. On the contrary, on New Year's Day 1589, she celebrated victory at Richmond Palace, giving expensive gifts to Lords Howard, Seymour and others. Nor did the queen lack loyalty. According to Garret Mattingly, 'Elizabeth was loyal to old friends. For a queen so notoriously fickle and changeable she changed her servants very seldom.'

Little had changed four hundred years later. In London's streets in 1920 you could find thousands of the men who had fought the War to

End War, many hideously injured or disfigured in both body and mind, jobless, homeless and begging at the roadside.

The lesson of these episodes is the same: that princes, governments and corporations only give any substantial reward to individuals who they favour, or who they cannot refuse. Those they can refuse, those they can forget, they will. Companies never give away anything they don't have to. This applies equally to employees and customers.

There is something of Mister Toad in mediaeval prince and modern corporations alike: Toad who will say anything, promise anything simply to get behind the wheel of a motor car once more and who will be without shame or conscience at making such promises because he never had any intention of keeping them.

It is as though the fact that a promise is impossible to keep absolves the promiser from any duty to attempt to stick to the spirit of his or her agreement. It is unreasonable, irrational, to expect someone to stick to a promise once it has become clear it cannot be kept. The more Peter ('Spycatcher') Wright insisted that he be given his MI5 pension, the more the government dug in its heels, regardless of the damage a disgruntled employee might cause them, merely by telling the truth.

Probably the exemplar without peer of the prince who acted purely from expediency was Henry VIII. When the Pope refused to divorce him, he removed him as head of the church, formed his own church and appointed himself instead. When his second wife, Ann Boleyn, refused to divorce him, he removed a head of quite another kind, again without conscience or scruple.

None of this behaviour compromised Henry's standing with his subjects because he always took care to ensure that he appeared to be acting in the interests of his country rather than merely himself.

As Niccolo Machiavelli put it: 'I conclude therefore that when a prince has the goodwill of the people he should not worry about conspiracies; but when the people are hostile and regard him with hatred he should go in fear of everything and everyone. Well-organised states and wise princes have always taken great pains not to exasperate the nobles, and to satisfy the people and keep them content; this is one of the most important tasks a prince must undertake.'

To which one can only add, how little things have changed in half a millennium of enlightened government.

How Perrier Lost its Mystique

Many of the examples given in this book could be considered simply as marketing mistakes in the sense that a flaw in the product precipitated a crisis in the market. In the case of France's best-known bottled water exporter, Source Perrier SA, it was a crisis in the market that exposed a flaw in the product: and showed that the company's management had adopted a novel approach to keeping its consumers happy.

Perrier's green bottle, with its hint of the saucy world of Henri Toulouse-Lautrec, is internationally famous and in the 1980s could be found on restaurant tables throughout Europe and America. The product had built up a reputation as a pure alternative to tap water, a reputation based on its natural sparkle and spring purity.[1]

Perrier extracts its famous water from a single natural spring at Vergeze, in southern France, and exports it everywhere, its label informing customers that it is 'naturally sparkling'.

The product was explained in the following way by Perrier US in its 1987 company report: 'One of Perrier's identifying qualities is its low mineral (particularly sodium) content. This is because the water spends only a short time filtering through minerals. While flowing underground, the water meets gas flowing vertically through porous volcanic rocks. This is how Perrier gets its fizz...the company assured us that production has never been limited by the source output. The company sells approximately one billion bottles of which 600 million are exported.'

Bottled water is big business. In its biggest export market, the United States, Perrier sold $800 million's worth of the product in 1989. Thus it was a bombshell when, at the beginning of February 1990, a local public health laboratory in North Carolina found traces of benzene, a carcinogen, in some bottles of Perrier, and reported these findings to the state health authorities. The state agriculture and health department announced the finding, warning that Perrier should not be drunk until further tests had been carried out.[2]

The president of Perrier US, Ronald Davis, acted the same day to allay public fears and announced that all 70 million bottles of Perrier would be withdrawn immediately from sale in North America as a precaution. The contamination was not serious – indeed the North Carolina authorities did not even issue a health advisory notice since the levels of benzene found did not pose any significant health risk. But the juxtaposition of Perrier's reputation for purity alongside contamination with benzene was a shocking discovery. It was not people's health at risk, it was Perrier's corporate image. Press and public alike wanted to know: how on earth could such a thing have happened? Was it sabotage?

The managing director of Source Perrier, Frederik Zimmer, made an immediate announcement at a press conference in Paris. The contamination had occurred, he said, because an employee whose job was to clean down production line machinery had mistakenly used a cleaning fluid containing benzene. However, the machinery had been stripped down over the weekend and thoroughly cleaned again. The production line was back in action as usual.[3]

The press hurried back to their offices to report the news that all was well with Perrier once more, and that the honour of France had been restored. Ominously, however, Ronald Davis held a simultaneous press conference in the United States during which he explained that Perrier would be off the market for 'two to three months'.

A week later, health authorities in Holland and Denmark announced that they, too, had found traces of benzene. Now Source Perrier recalled not just its North American output but Perrier worldwide. A second press conference was called in Paris. This time Frederik Zimmer and his fellow directors told a different story.

It wasn't just one production line that had been contaminated by traces of benzene in recent months, said Zimmer, but all Perrier production. The reason, he said, was that benzene occurs naturally in all Perrier water but that workers had failed to replace filters designed to remove it. Nor was this all, for Perrier water contained several gases of which benzene was one, all of which had to be filtered out.

This was a radically different story from the previous press conference. It was no longer the gormless youth with an oily rag, alone in the factory at night, carelessly swabbing down the production line: now Perrier was apparently admitting to a problem intrinsic to its production process. The company insisted that its spring was pure and unpolluted but their announcement left many unanswered questions hanging in the air. Was the benzene man-made or naturally occurring? Was it a harmless natural substance or pollution that resulted from some nearby industrial processes?

In the end the questions became so numerous that the company was compelled to come clean about its famous water. Perrier water does not simply bubble up from the ground, pure and 'naturally sparkling' and ready to drink. Instead, the company extracts the water and carbon dioxide gas separately, pipes the gas through charcoal filters to remove benzene and other impurities, and then combines them in its bottling plant. If the filters failed, or were not present, the resulting water would contain benzene and other gases and would taste like rotten eggs.

In the following months, Perrier production and distribution returned to normal, but market conditions have never returned to those before the benzene affair came to light. It was five months later, in July 1990, before Perrier was fully available in all its markets once more. The company spent prodigiously on advertising to rebuild lost sales. In the US alone it spent $16 million on advertising and another $9 million on marketing and special events.

Perhaps most surprising of all during the lay-off was the Perrier board's cavalier attitude to the affair, which it saw as merely a storm in a water glass. President Frederik Zimmer told one journalist, 'all this publicity helps build the brand's renown'.[4]

The reality was somewhat different. The US Federal Food and Drug Administration made the company remove the words 'naturally sparkling' from its bottle labels.

The increased advertising expenditure could not prevent competitors moving in to fill the vacuum left by a five-month absence from the market. Perrier's French rival, Evian, took over as the top-selling brand of imported bottled water in the United States and elsewhere by the end of 1990. New entrants to the market, such as own-brand supermarket water, were encouraged by Perrier's absence to expand their market share.

Perrier hoped to return to 85 per cent of its previous sales level by the end of the year, but it managed only 60 per cent. In the US its share of the bottle water market sank from nearly 45 per cent a year earlier to only 21 per cent, though it has climbed slowly since. Much of the lost sales were with restaurants and bars, which started to offer Evian from France, Spa from Belgium and Pellagrino from Italy. Labels from little known springs all over England and Scotland started to appear on supermarket shelves.

Perhaps the most extraordinary thing about the whole affair was that the contamination itself was trivial and harmless. It was its effect in lifting the lid on Perrier's guilty secret that was so damaging.

CHAPTER FOURTEEN

THE SHELL GAME
How to deal successfully with companies...*and how Hoover got sucked in*

Large corporations have a built-in advantage over their customers. It is not an inner moral strength or Bhuddic serenity; not their financial soundness or their technological expertise. It is that, like the street gamblers who fleece punters with the shell game, or 'Find the Lady', they know the moves we will make before we make them, because they have seen them all many, many times before.

It is not that they are smarter than us, merely that they are better informed by virtue of their position as a supplier.

Ford and General Motors know to the month how long we will keep our cars before changing them; McVitie's know to the last biscuit how many chocolate digestives will be dipped in cups of tea on a Wednesday afternoon; Guinness know how many bottles of Irish Stout will disappear down British throats on Derby Day.

The success of companies in predicting our behaviour arises simply from their having a sample of many thousands of transactions on which to base their judgement.

Similarly, the key to dealing successfully with companies is being able to predict their behaviour just as they are able to predict ours. Fortunately, unlike corporations, we do not need to have a sample of thousands in order to have a representative cross-section. This is because in the personality factors that really matter – the unconscious factors – large organisations virtually all react in the same way.

As we have seen in earlier chapters, most corporations are thin-skinned, ultra-sensitive, highly prone to cognitive dissonance, hate surprises, and are willing to believe that their employees and customers are powerless. Many will say anything and do anything to sell their products and services or save their skins if they are caught out in dirty deeds. They are childishly transparent when they try to deceive, yet, at the same time, they are notoriously careless of their corporate image because they are self-deluding about how they are perceived. The typical corporation is a jellyfish that thinks it's an armadillo; a raddled harridan who thinks she's an attractive young girl.

One important company characteristic that we have so far not looked at in any detail is how a company's management react when their plans, their theories, their market predictions all turn out to be wrong. What exactly happens when the confident predictions made by senior corporate managers fail to come true? How can the chief executive and the rest of the board survive when their plans fail to materialise? Are they not immediately and irrevocably discredited? Strangely, this happens only very rarely. What happens in such cases is explained by Leon Festinger in his book *When Prophecy Fails*.

Festinger and his colleagues, Henry Riecken and Stanley Schachter, carried out a study of just this question at the Laboratory for Research in Social Relations at the University of Minnesota.[1]

'Suppose', said Festinger, 'an individual believes something with his whole heart; suppose further that he has a commitment to this belief, that he has taken irrevocable actions because of it; finally, suppose that he is presented with evidence, unequivocal and undeniable evidence that his belief is wrong: what will happen?'

The answer, says Festinger, is that 'the individual will frequently emerge, not only unshaken, but even more convinced of the truth of his beliefs than ever before. Indeed, he may even show a new fervour about convincing and converting other people to his view.'

Festinger's fascinating study was conducted with a group of individuals who believed they were receiving messages from alien beings regarding a planned landing on earth that would precipitate a second coming of the messiah and bring about cataclysmic events. As we will see later, this

141

unpromisingly eccentric material is of direct relevance to anyone who wishes to understand corporate behaviour.

In the course of studying these beliefs and the outcome of the group's actions, Festinger was able to document the effects of unequivocal disconfirmation of the group's main prediction – the non-appearance of flying saucers and the non-occurrence of a flood of biblical proportions – on a group of twenty-six people who had come to believe in the reality of the messages from outer space.

The group had formed spontaneously over a period of time around a Minnesota woman, Mrs Marian Keech. Mrs Keech claimed to be receiving automatic writings from a spiritual being called Ananda. The people Mrs Keech attracted were by no means poorly educated or easily suggestible. They included Dr Thomas Armstrong, a physician and college lecturer, and his wife; and Dr Clyde Wilton, a research scientist with a post at a major research institution and a respected member of the scientific profession. There was also the director of a nursery school, several teachers and a large number of students, including postgraduates studying science and sociology. There was also a strong religious thread running through the group, which called itself The Seekers.

In essence, the messages told The Seekers that there would be a great flood in which unbelievers would perish. Members of the Seekers, however, would be directed to safe places on high ground where flying saucers would land and transport them to another planet. Members of the group would be considered worthy of being saved by the flying saucers only if they gave away all their worldly goods and purified themselves through prayer.

Eventually, the Guardians divulged to Mrs Keech the date of this event: it was to take place on the 21 December next. Dr Armstrong passed this information to the local newspaper, which ran a two-column story on its back page, headlined: PROPHECY FROM PLANET CLARION CALL TO CITY: FLEE THAT FLOOD. IT'LL SWAMP US ON DEC 21, OUTER SPACE TELLS SUBURBANITE.

The story revealed that, 'Lake City will be destroyed by a flood from Great Lake just before dawn December 21, according to a suburban housewife. Mrs Marian Keech of 847 West School Street, says the prophecy is not her own. It is the purport of many messages she has received by automatic writing, she says... The messages, according to Mrs Keech, are sent to her by superior beings from a planet called "Clarion". These beings have been visiting the earth, she says, in what we call flying saucers. During their visits, she says, they have observed fault lines in the earth's crust that foretoken the deluge. Mrs Keech reports she was told the flood will spread to form an inland sea stretching from the Arctic Circle to the Gulf of Mexico. At the same time, she says, a cataclysm will submerge the West Coast from Seattle, Wash., to Chile in South America.'

As the date drew near, the group became nervous. The senior members urged the younger Seekers not to panic; to keep their nerve and remain ready for the imminent deluge. The appointed day arrived and was taken up by Mrs Keech giving interviews to local radio stations and newspaper reporters. There was, however, no flood and no arrival of flying saucers.

In their observations of the group members following the non-event, the researchers found that the great majority – all except two or three individuals who, for various reasons, were only weakly attached to the group – believed in the space beings and their imminent arrival even more strongly than before. A stream of new prophecies were issued and dozens of interviews given to press and radio. New dates were set for the landings but these also came and went with no spacemen. Still The Seekers kept on seeking.

How is the behaviour of a group that most people would regard as a bunch of crackpots relevant to that of the directors of a public corporation? The answer is in the essential conditions that Festinger proposed: that there must be conviction; that there must be commitment to this conviction; that the conviction must be amenable to unequivocal disconfirmation; that such disconfirmation must then occur.

Although drawn up with cult believers in mind, the criteria are a perfect match for many a corporate boardroom: Coca-Cola and new Coke; IBM and its PS/2; Intel and the Pentium; Benetton and its ad campaign; Disney and its European theme park.

All had a burning conviction of the rightness of their decision and their planned course of action. All made very significant commitments to that belief: investing millions of dollars; committing major corporate resources of personnel and machinery; staking the corporate reputation and share price on a successful outcome. All received unequivocal disconfirmation: only 13 per cent of those polled liked new Coke, 84 per cent preferred something else; PC buyers bought tens of millions of PCs from clone makers, not IBM; only a minority of loyal corporate customers bought PS/2 and practically no one bought OS/2; Intel customers refused to buy the faulty Pentium chip or else demanded replacement; Benetton's own retailers sued them for loss of earnings; tourists brought their own packed lunch and wine to Disneyland Paris with its expensive, alcohol-free, fast food bars.

Yet in each case, even with unequivocal disconfirmation inescapably before them in the sales figures, the board continued for months to insist that its original belief had been correct; it was the customers who were wrong; just another few millions on advertising and marketing and the customers will wake up and realise the mistake they have made. Hence Coca-Cola's twin-track advertising scheme; Intel's Internet messages of encouragement; IBM's video films extolling its product's merits; Benetton's insistence on running its ads regardless of industry warnings; Disney pressing ahead even when the protesters were telling it unambiguously to 'Go home'.

The only reason that large corporations have got away with so much for so long is not because their behaviour has been cleverly self-protective. On the contrary, as examples in earlier chapters show, most corporations' behaviour is characterised by incompetence and self-delusion. It is not fox-like cunning that has saved companies, merely the fact that their customers have hardly begun to wake up to the fact that they can influence their suppliers with every bit as much power as their suppliers influence them.

As a result, corporations that have had virtually a free hand for decades are beginning to encounter stiffer and stiffer opposition, and it is beginning to hurt them – though some of the sources of this opposition are, if anything, even more worrying than the corporations themselves.

In the United States, for instance, a Mississippi preacher, Don Wildmon, has formed the American Family Association, an organisation aimed at forcing corporations not to promote on television what Wildmon and his members regard as depravity. So far, the Association has attracted no less than two million members and by mobilising their spending power to boycott products in the shops, Wildmon has frightened off companies like Pepsi and K-Mart.

The AFA supports what Wildmon calls 'traditional family values'. In 1991, his organisation targeted US discount retail chain K-Mart because they said a subsidiary, Waldenbooks, was carrying pornography on its shelves. AFA members began to boycott the stores and sales dropped. When Pepsi planned a multi-million dollar advertising campaign with Madonna, Wildmon's organisation threatened a similar boycott and the campaign has been shelved.

Wildmon says, 'I have just one motivation – to protect the family. This country was built on the family. In the past 30 years, family values have been under attack. During that time crime has risen, illegitimacy has risen, drug abuse is all but out of control. That's what happens when the family is weakened.'

Wildmon blames the marketing policies of large corporations for contributing to this collapse of values and is organising what he sees as a campaign to fight back. Now the AFA is even turning its attention to British companies who are advertising on US television. In 1995, the AFA targeted Unilever because it had placed commercials either side of *NYPD Blue*, thus, according to the Association, 'promoting depravity'.

'Unilever's support of *NYPD Blue* is helping to open the doors of sexual nudity on prime time TV,' says Wildmon. 'America was built on the family; *NYPD Blue* is undermining the family. We won't stand by and let that happen.'

The AFA has sent out plastic boycott cards to its members. The cards are designed to fit neatly into the shopper's purse or wallet and list all of Unilever's household products, so that members know which products to leave on the shelves when visiting the supermarket. Given that there are two million members, this threat is not inconsiderable and Unilever is worried.

Wildmon says, 'I've seen a confidential Unilever memo. It was sent out by Ronald Goldstein, the president of Unilever US. He said the whole *NYPD Blue* series of advertisements is under review. Senior staff were asked to comment on how best to handle a withdrawal.'

The existence of Wildmon's organisation is disturbing to most people because of its threat to freedom of speech. Marjorie Heims of the American Civil Liberties Union, for instance, says, 'Wildmon is a threat to liberty. He is trying to accomplish censorship which runs right against the spirit of the First Amendment.'

Fortunately, there are no signs of a Wildmon in the UK and it is hard to imagine his brand of Southern religious fervour catching on in Bradford or Bournemouth. But what the success of the AFA shows is that, given the right conditions, people can be mobilised to oppose large corporations successfully with remarkably little effort – a plastic card listing products to be boycotted is enough to do the trick. The 'right conditions' include the strong feelings engendered by personal opposition to some aspect of corporate behaviour.

The effect is reminiscent of the ease with which Shell's customers were able to make the company change its mind about dumping Brent Spar. An important aspect of the Shell boycott that will not be lost on the company's directors or its competitors is how easy it was for its customers to change their buying habits once their threshold of outrage was reached. Most of us prefer to continue to shop in the same way at the same outlets as a matter of routine, regardless of marginal variations in price and service: familiarity being more important than quality and price. But once a customer decides to break his or her habit and look elsewhere, it is usually not too difficult to find cheaper or better alternatives.

How many of its customers it has lost for good is something that Shell will not know for some time to come, as the Brent Spar incident is gradually forgotten, old habits reassert themselves, and customers drift back. But the company will be awaiting the final score with some trepidation, because it is possible that it has lost a small but significant fraction of its revenue for good and that it will prove difficult to replace without great effort and expense.

How Hoover Got Sucked In

Hoover has manufactured vacuum cleaners in Britain for almost a hundred years but business is not what it used to be in the 1960s, when Harold MacMillan told British consumers that they had 'never had it so good'.[2] In 1992, the firm's factory in the Scottish village of Cambuslang, near Glasgow, was on a three-day week. But in scenes that could have come straight from an Ealing comedy, the sleepy village and its factory were about to be galvanised into activity as never before.

In August 1992, Hoover's marketing department came up with a promotion scheme worthy of P T Barnum. If you bought more than £100 worth of Hoover products before the end of January 1993, you could get two return air tickets to one of a number of European destinations. If you bought £250 worth of Hoover products, you could have two free return air tickets to New York or Orlando, Florida.[3]

On the face of it the offer was too good to be true: Hoover seemed to be giving away more than they were getting. In fact, the promotion was one of a type that is quite common. Hoover had done a deal with two travel agencies. The agencies would supply 'space-available' seats on airlines at low cost. These are the remaining empty seats that are available on many flights and are sold at heavily reduced prices through agents to fill them up.

Moreover, the people taking up the offer would not merely need airline seats, they would also need hotel accommodation, rental cars and insurance. The agents would sell a package deal to those people taking up the air travel offer and Hoover would get a commission on each package: the more people who took up the offer, the more commissions Hoover would get. On paper, Hoover couldn't lose.

Whatever the economics of the arrangement, British home owners could recognise a good deal when they saw one and tens of thousands of them rushed to the high streets and stripped the shelves bare of Hoover products. For a time, it was literally impossible to buy a Hoover vacuum cleaner anywhere in Britain.

The village of Cambuslang hummed night and day as workers at the Hoover factory came off their three-day week and were put onto a 24-hour, 7-days a week production schedule, frantically trying to re-stock the stores in the high street where the buying frenzy continued unabated. For the first few weeks, the marketing department congratulated itself on a brilliant idea. Then things started to go wrong.

When it had drawn up its promotional plan, Hoover had estimated that fewer than 50,000 would respond to it and of these, far fewer would bother to go through all the steps necessary to qualify for free travel and actually book a flight – perhaps 5,000 or 10,000 people.

In the event more than 200,000 not only responded, but also booked a holiday. Disneyworld in Orlando was a particularly popular destination for families with young children. However, most of these 200,000 declined to purchase a package deal with Hoover, preferring to shop around elsewhere for cheap hotel accommodation and car rental, hence Hoover received few commissions.

But the sheer volume of people taking up the offer overwhelmed the company. A huge administrative bottleneck was created with more and more people buying products and demanding air tickets, but fewer and fewer people actually travelling. By April 1993, only around 6,000 people had actually flown anywhere.

Tens of thousands wrote in for their tickets, but never received them, or couldn't get the flight dates or destinations they wanted. Many wrote in but heard nothing for months. Soon Hoover was receiving calls from irate customers at the rate of 2,000 a day and had to set up a hotline just to deal with them.

Frustration turned to anger as disgruntled customers began to accuse Hoover of incompetence and even fraud. The press got onto the story and the name Hoover started to appear regularly in the financial and City pages with accounts of the débâcle. They got a picture story as well when one customer held a Hoover van hostage. The *Sunday Times* reported: 'One disgruntled customer, who took aggressive action on his own, received the widest press coverage, and even became a folk hero. Dave

Dixon, claiming he was cheated out of a free holiday by Hoover, seized one of the company's repair vans in retaliation. Police were sympathetic: they took him home, and did not charge him, claiming it was a civil matter.'[4]

It was at this point that things became too much for Hoover's American parent company, Maytag Corporation. Maytag had acquired Hoover only four years before. Now they were saddled with huge unexpected losses that were self-inflicted. Maytag dispatched several senior directors to Britain who promptly sacked three Hoover executives involved in the promotion, including the president of Hoover Europe.

They then set about trying to sort out the mess. It cost them $30 million in the first quarter of 1993 to cover unexpected costs associated with the promotion and, in the end, the total bill was nearer $50 million. This was an amount equivalent to ten per cent of Hoover's total UK revenue.

The problem with the promotional idea is easy enough to see with hindsight: Hoover should have placed some kind of limit on the number of applications it would accept, perhaps the first 5,000 or 10,000. But the cause of the disaster is also not far to seek. The company had persuaded itself that it knew in advance how people would react: that customers' natural apathy would limit the number of applications it received. The prophecy to which they became so strongly attached was wrong.

So far we have seen a wide variety of pathological behaviour from organisations of all kinds; some harmful to employees, some harmful to customers and some, as here, harmful to the organisation itself. But if this kind of behaviour is really so common, how do large companies ever make any money?

CHAPTER FIFTEEN

LUCK OF THE DEVIL
How companies succeed despite themselves...*and how banks print their own money*

If the hallmark of many large organisations is incompetence and inefficiency, as this book proposes, it is reasonable to ask: how does it come about that there are so many large, wealthy organisations, capable of making big profits for their shareholders, providing much-needed employment and contributing a healthy slice of their revenue to the country as taxation? Surely this financial and managerial success is testament to the competence and efficiency of Britain's commercial companies?

It doesn't take much analysis to see that the reality is rather different. As discussed earlier, many companies are successful not because of the quality of their management, but because of just a few factors that are entirely beyond the day-to-day control of its executives: possession of a monopoly or near monopoly; an insatiable demand for the company's products or services; or having a very wide margin between costs and prices, for instance due to low cost of raw materials or labour.

With few exceptions, the most successful commercial companies are those who – regardless of the quality of their management, and whatever rationalisations are contained in their business plans and their annual reports – have cashed in successfully on one or more of these external factors.

For example, of the top 50 most profitable companies in Britain in one recent *Times* list, ten sell the addictive drugs tobacco and alcohol (British American Tobacco, Grand Metropolitan, Guinness, Rothmans, Allied-

150

Lyons, Bass, Argyll, Gallaher, Whitbread and Scottish & Newcastle); ten sell oil, gas, petrol, electricity or water (Shell, British Gas, National Power, National Grid, Esso, PowerGen, Severn Trent, Scottish Power, Thames Water and North West Water); five make or sell foods through supermarket chains (Sainsbury, Unilever, Tesco, Weston Holdings and Cadbury Schweppes); four sell drugs and medicines (Glaxo, SmithKline Beecham, Wellcome and Boots); three sell staple products through high street chain stores (Marks & Spencer, Great Universal and Kingfisher) and three are high street banks. Also, of the same top 50 companies, 13 are monopolies or virtual monopolies (British Telecom, British Gas, Cable & Wireless, National Power, National Grid, PowerGen, Vodafone, Severn Trent, Scottish Power, Post Office, Thames Water, North West Water and British Airports Authority). Only a small minority (perhaps six or seven out of 50) are companies who could reasonably claim to have become successful primarily because of their management effectiveness, and even here their very large size grants them monopoly-like influence in some respects.

Take banks for example. Typically, banks enjoy all three of the natural advantages needed for a successful company: they enjoy a near monopoly because of stringent licensing requirements (though this is slowly being eroded); their charges are high, they have low administrative running costs and computerisation has enabled them continually to reduce their payroll; and there is an insatiable demand for their product – money.

Even though they have – almost literally – a license to print money, the high street banks are unable to produce a return on capital employed of much more than one per cent – only a tenth of the norm for any other industry, as the illustrative cases described later demonstrate.

The fact that banking provides a license to print money is obvious even to the casual observer as its product is money. What is rather less obvious is that the same is true of most of Britain's largest companies. Regardless of its product or service, any company has a license to print money if it has a monopoly or near monopoly of its market, like the energy or communications vendors; or if it deals in products for which demand is insatiable such as tobacco, alcohol, petrol, pharmaceuticals, energy, water, or staple foods; or if it is able to buy cheap and sell dear without any special negotiating skill, as in the case of the water utilities.

The point to realise about such organisations is that because of their built-in capacity to attract revenue, there is no market discipline or compulsion upon them to manage their businesses efficiently. This is very different from saying that they do not strive to do so, of course, and many of Britain's large companies have become a byword for their efforts to instil managerial efficiency in their staff. But the point is, if the company's revenue stream is big enough and strong enough, it doesn't matter whether its management is efficient or not: the bottom line of its financial results will still have a very big number in the space marked 'net profit'. The city, the shareholders and the press will accept the organisation at face value as a corporate lion in the commercial jungle even if, in reality, the organisation is more like a corporate slug wandering in an unguarded lettuce patch.

It is only fair to repeat that the fact that a company enjoys a naturally high volume of sales and a high margin on those sales does not mean that its management is lazy or inefficient, but it does mean that its management doesn't have to be energetic or efficient and that it won't get into trouble even if it is found to be lacking in expertise. This is a warning signal of ideal conditions for stimulating ineffectual corporate behaviour.

How Banks Print their Own Money

By law, the high street banks such as Barclays, Lloyds, NatWest and HSBC, are licensed to lend eight times the amount they hold on deposit, at the prevailing rate of interest. The real rate of return, after inflation, is generally around six per cent. In theory, this means that a bank that takes in, say, £25 billion in deposits can lend £200 billion at six per cent, which yields a gross income of £12,000 million.

Of course, there are many things that can go wrong with this scenario and make a substantial dent in profits. Demand for loans can fluctuate and the bank may not be able to lend all its resources at the best rate. There are bad debts to provide for and, like all businesses, banking has high costs – for people, for premises and for equipment. Even so, any reasonable person would expect that if a business had our imaginary £200 billion of working capital at its disposal, it would be able to make significant profits. Yet the banks signally fail to do so.

Take Barclays, for example. In the fiscal year 2000, Barclays did have 'interest receivable' of almost £12 billion, just as in our imaginary example above. This must mean that it took deposits somewhere in the region of £25 billion, allowing it in turn to loan something like £200 billion.[1]

Yet Barclays' profit before tax in fiscal 2000 was 'only' £3,496 million. To put this in perspective: in having up to £200 billion to lend, Barclays was able to make less than £3.5 billion – only 1.8 per cent return on capital employed.

Much the same is true if you look at Barclays' balance sheet and compare its assets with its earnings. Total assets of Barclays was £316 billion. So the company employed capital assets of more than £316 billion just to make a profit of less than £3.5 billion – again a return on capital employed of little over one per cent.

In industry generally, target profitability on capital employed is around ten per cent. Barclay's profitability was only one tenth of the norm.

To make this clearer, Barclays spent more than 98 per cent of the money paid in across its counters in handling and accounting for that money. Had that income been tens of millions, this level of inefficiency would have been disturbing; had the income been hundreds of millions then it would have been cause for concern. In fact, that income was tens of thousands of millions, leading one to wonder what income the bank would have to have before it could show a profitability anywhere near industry norms.

Barclays are not alone in having such a poor profit record. Lloyds TSB, NatWest and HSBC are all in the same boat. All handle tens of billions in deposits each year.

Yet despite having so much money pass through their hands, very little of it sticks to their fingers. Of course, it seems strange to use the phrase 'poor profit record' of a company that makes profits of nearly £3,500 million in a single year. But the huge sum on the bottom line tends to obscure the real facts and lead us to conclude that the high street banks are highly profitable and efficiently run.

Another example of the high street banks' inefficiency is the way in which they have collectively spent hundreds of millions of pounds on ineffective or badly implemented computer systems. In a counting house, the one thing that you can be reasonably sure of automating is the counting; hence computers have been the mainstay of developments in banking for decades.

Banking is historically a labour-intensive industry, needing fingers to count and brains to add up and check the figures. Computers have been the one instrument that has enabled banks to reduce dramatically the number of people needed to handle money and do their accounting. This process of automation has been proceeding at an accelerating pace for three decades, with hundreds of thousands of banking jobs replaced by tireless machines, working uncomplainingly around the clock, without tea breaks, salary negotiations or maternity leave.

Wave after wave of redundancies have been made by the banks since the 1960s, each one in the name of greater efficiency and cost savings that would make the banks more competitive, and hence more profitable. After decades of such efforts, the banks must by now be as lean and mean and profitable as it is possible for them to get. Yet few of them are able to turn in a performance of much over one per cent return on capital employed – five to ten times worse than the norm in any other industry. One can only wonder what state the banks would have been in had they not made the staff cuts of the last 30 years.

CHAPTER SIXTEEN

BOOTLEGGERS AND SPEAKEASIES
How some companies get it right…and how H-P fixed a multi-million dollar bug

Poor performance may be the norm when one is wandering around the foothills and valleys of the corporate world, but the occasional glimpse of a sunlit peak can more than make up for the disappointment of the daily grind. Some organisations stand out in the crowd because they have adopted unusual, imaginative, creative policies that inspire great things from their employees; others stand out simply because they have decided to do the right thing in a world where most people decide not to bother.

Earlier, I pointed to the inability of some companies to innovate successfully, even when they have done so in the past. One obstacle to creative innovation is the bureaucratic obsession with accountability for R and D funding. If a corporate researcher is going to get into trouble for using up scarce funds chasing a pot of gold at the end of what turns out to be an illusory rainbow, then it is hardly surprising that some companies' research departments become 'bloated bureaucracies' that fail to innovate.

Some organisations have recognised this danger and acted to minimise its effects. Adhesives and coatings company 3M has introduced a policy of allowing its researchers to spend 15 per cent of their time on 'bootleg' research – the kind of wild ideas that otherwise have to be kept hidden away in a desk drawer in case anyone sees them. As a result of this policy, 3M came up with one of its all-time best-selling products.

In the early 1970s, one of its scientists, Dr Spencer Silver, discovered what seemed at the time a pointless material – an adhesive that didn't stick, or an 'unglue'. The material was actually an adhesive that had 'low tack', meaning that it did not bond tightly with the surface with which it came in contact but peeled away without leaving any residue. The material was unusual but had no application that anyone could think of – it was a solution looking for a problem.

In 1974, another 3M employee, chemical engineer Arthur Fry, came up with the problem. Fry spent each Sunday singing for the choir in his local church and used to mark the pages in his hymn-book with scraps of paper that kept falling out. Wouldn't it be great, thought Fry, if there was such a thing as a sticky bookmark that wouldn't fall out?

Fry recalled his colleague's 'unglue', and as a piece of 'bootleg' research, experimented with applying it to a handy-sized scrap of paper. The result was the 'Post-it' note that is now stuck to a million PC screens and Filofaxes every day. Even when Fry had perfected his invention, it still nearly succumbed to the 'not invented here – no one wants it' syndrome.

3M test-marketed the yellow Post-it notes, but few people bought them since they couldn't see what need they fulfilled. The invention would probably have died a quiet death had it not been for the fact that an unusually persistent 3M marketing executive noticed that although overall sales were poor, sales had been very good in a small number of areas. The unknown executive then checked and found that the high sales had been achieved in areas where free samples had been handed out first. Once people had tried them, they were hooked. Post-it notes are now one of 3M's five best-selling products along with Scotch tape.

Another company to address basic issues of human communication, not just in its brochures but also in its structure, is Avis, the car rental company. As described earlier, Avis insists that everyone who joins the company, even at board level, has to stand behind the counter of the familiar Avis kiosk at an airport or similar public venue and deal with the harassed business people who pass through, looking to rent a car in a hurry. Supermarket chain Safeway has a similar rule about promoting managerial staff only from the shop floor, so that people on the board understand what it means to stack tins of beans.

How Hewlett-Packard Fixed a Multi-million Dollar Bug

One fine morning in 1995, people all over Europe opened the door to the postman and were handed a small but weighty parcel that none of them was expecting. Having signed for it and looked inside, full of curiosity, these puzzled recipients found that it contained a well-engineered and well-made mechanism together with a diskette containing software, a little manual in six languages, and a letter of explanation from Hewlett-Packard's European general manager.

In the previous couple of years, millions of people around the world had bought a Hewlett-Packard deskjet printer. There had, said the letter, been some reports of the friction wheels that feed the paper into these printers becoming worn. The enclosed device had been designed and manufactured and was being sent free of charge to purchasers of the printers to resurface the feed wheels in case they did wear.

The cost of this exercise to deal with what appears to be an almost trivial defect must have been staggering. Postage alone must have been millions. Manufacturing the devices must have cost more millions. Why on earth should any company, even a big one like H-P, voluntarily pay millions to fix such a small bug? What exactly made it worthwhile?

Most people will have noticed how many offices use Hewlett-Packard laser or inkjet printers. But how many are aware that the printer business is worth $10 billion a year worldwide and that Hewlett-Packard owns 60 per cent of that market? The company was acting to protect annual revenues of around $6 billion.

Hewlett-Packard is America's ninth largest multinational corporation with sales of more than $41 billion in 2000. Its name is probably best known in offices throughout the world because of its laser and inkjet computer printers, but the firm sells many other electronic products: industrial electronic equipment, laboratory equipment, computers and calculators.

In the best tradition of the American dream, its founders started their company over a garage in downtown California in the postwar electronics boom. They decided to charge a lot for their products, but they also decided to back this high price policy with high levels of quality and after sales service.

Problems like H-P's printer bug occur in most manufacturing companies (and even some service organisations) from time to time. The fault crops up only in a minority of products, perhaps depending on how much or how roughly they are used. The fault is minor in that it does not prevent operation completely but impedes it in some slight way. Complex devices, such as computers and their printers, domestic appliances and motor cars often have minor problems of this sort associated with them. In many cases, the owner has to work around the problem.

In cases where the fault is potentially dangerous – usually where it affects electrical wiring or poor earthing – the manufacturer has little choice but to advertise in the press recalling the suspect device for repair. But where it is in the nature of a nuisance rather than dangerous, many manufacturers decide that the least said, soonest mended. Most of us have owned equipment that is faulty in this minor way and have grumbled about it but soldiered on.

Understandably, if the fault is trivial, most companies will decide to take no action. As described in the case of Intel and the Pentium chip, the rational course of action seems to be to sit tight, volunteer nothing and offer to replace the defective unit only if anyone kicks up a fuss. In many cases, this strategy may well work. The problem with it from a corporate image standpoint is that its outcome is entirely unpredictable. Perhaps more importantly, as Intel discovered, it can have very damaging effects on the organisation's credibility, and once that is lost, there is nothing the organisation can do in the short term to regain it.

But the main problem with this approach from the company's point of view is that everything will be all right only as long as customers with the faulty product don't find out about each other and get together. If even half a dozen customers find they have the same problem, then the supplier is in big trouble: it will inevitably look as if it has been conspiring to keep quiet and as if it doesn't really care about customer satisfaction (regardless of what the clever marketing consultants write in the company brochures). Most serious of all, it may well be open to harmful exposure in the press and possibly even a class action for damages.

Somebody, somewhere in Hewlett-Packard recognised this, and to their credit decided to do something about it before the company's reputation was damaged. The result of this decision to bite the bullet and pay to put the defect right was the gizmo brought by the postman.

That is the rational explanation for the contents of the postman's sack: that Hewlett-Packard was avoiding bad publicity, the possibility of lawsuits and protecting its market share. But there is also its unconscious motivation. No one *made* the company spend millions. In this unforced action we are seeing what the company is really like. And what it is really like is someone who believes in looking after its paying customers.

CHAPTER SEVENTEEN

A SUITABLE CASE FOR TREATMENT
How sick companies can be treated

If an individual behaved in the way that many of the corporations described in this book behaved, then we would have little hesitation in advising them to seek professional help. Imagine the local fish shop owner deciding to drop his usual menu of cod or haddock and serving his customers goldfish or dolphin instead, and you have some idea of the nature of Coca-Cola's actions on a personal level. Or picture the local garage proprietor disposing of his old fuel pumps by dumping them in the park's ornamental lake and you get an idea of what Shell's behaviour means on an individual basis.

At the very least we would advise these people to have a serious talk with a business counsellor; more likely we would suggest that they see a psychiatrist to get themselves sorted out. But what can a corporation do when it is sick? There are as yet no company psychiatrists to turn to – though I predict that corporate psychiatry is likely to become a crowded profession in future.

Corporate health is already big business. Hundreds of millions are spent each year on management consultants; on seminars, training courses, books and videos. But the object of this expenditure, the patient who is the target of this attention, is always conceived as a rational adult amenable to reason.

The consultant's recommendations, the seminar's acronyms, the video's comedic dramatisations, are all aimed at managers who are part of a mature organisation, open to rational debate and willing to change. Few have imagined that the corporation to whom they are trying to appeal rationally might not be an adult at all but a naughty schoolboy with chocolate round his mouth, or, even worse, a teenage sociopath with a flick knife in his pocket and a chip on his shoulder: as unscrupulous and anti-social as the street gangs of New York.

It has become fashionable to analyse the main activities of an industrial or commercial corporation in terms of business processes – manufacturing, distribution, marketing and so on – and to speak in terms of re-engineering those processes, much as one would re-tool the factory production line for a new model of car.

It is easy to overlook the fact that the organisation *itself* is a process: a process in which resources are transformed by information. In this case, however, it is a process in which the transformation of those resources is mediated by the mind of the company: a mind that has an unconscious component that tends to interfere with the corporate decision-making process, with the kind of malignant results that are the subject of this book.

Thus the psychology of the organisation plays a dominant role in the transformation of its resources and re-engineering the process is not merely a matter of re-tooling; it is a matter of corporate psychoanalysis, a matter of techniques not from the shop floor but from the analyst's consulting room. What we are here considering is the psychopathology of the corporation: the company as sociopath.

The process nature of organisations is far from obvious. Corporations dislike thinking of themselves as anything so ephemeral and strive first and foremost to impress the rest of us with their solidity and permanence – just look at the headquarters buildings of Shell at Waterloo, IBM at Portsmouth or NatWest in the City, compare them with the Pharaonic glory of Egypt's middle kingdom and you will see how their minds are working.

Yet the true nature of companies as commercially transient processes is revealed when time is telescoped and their achievements are viewed all at once. As we saw earlier, IBM was never really a great computer company: merely a successful one.

IBM was never great in the sense of being a centre of excellence in the way that Rolls-Royce is a great engine maker and developer. On the contrary, it sought to stifle the innovations that could have ensured its continued dominance. IBM was simply the steward for a brief time of the mainframe business, a vacancy it engaged at the fortuitous moment because of the positioning given it by Thomas Watson Jr in the business machine market, the historical precursor of the computer market.

Similarly, it could be argued that DuPont has never been a great chemical company, it was merely the organisation that employed the genius of Wallace Carothers and hence became the temporary steward of nylon – again an opportune engagement.

The number of companies that have had more than one blockbuster product can be counted on the fingers of one hand. In the overwhelming majority of cases, companies are successful because of a single invention: the Hughes drilling bit; nylon; the pneumatic tyre; celluloid film; xerography; the transistor.

Equally, in many cases, the successful company is the one who was first in the field: Dunlop; Xerox; Kodak; Polaroid; Fairchild. Yet this achievement – laudable though it is – is nothing to do with the men and women who in the past managed and today manage the corporation in its developed state. It is thanks to the innovator who started the company in a skunk works: John Dunlop; George Eastman; Edwin Land, Chester Carlson, Robert Shockley. (Perhaps the main exception here is Henry Ford, whose chief invention was not the motor car itself but the means of mass producing it: the factory production line and the single-piece casting of parts like the cylinder block.)

In the overwhelming majority of cases, companies are not eminent because of the kind of qualities that they talk about at seminars and write about in their brochures – flexibility, innovation, responsiveness, and all the rest. They are eminent because chance has dealt them a single winning card, usually in the form of a product advantage, geographical advantage or historical advantage, that they have hung onto for a decade or two, before being overtaken by other companies. They were as much victims of fate when they were dealt the winning card as they are victims of fate when they are dealt the one that says their day is done and their leadership a thing of the past.

But just what is it that acts to *prevent* corporations from repeating their earlier success – given their access to capital and talent?

In many cases, the main reason is that the corporation dares not consciously enquire too closely into the reasons for its initial success, because to do so would be to confront the devastating knowledge that its success was purely fortuitous and that it is beyond its powers to repeat that success at will. No corporation wishes to learn that its success was no more than being in the right place at the right time and that all its management posturing since has been no more than the *post hoc* rationalisation of a lucky break.

Like people, companies suffer from infantile amnesia: they shut away the truth about their origins, preferring to remain in ignorance so they can continue to believe that their success is due to factors within their control. This is why, in general, large corporations have so little *real* knowledge about the identity and motives of their customers, and why those customers buy the products or services they buy.

In some companies, this amnesia expresses itself in the fact that the board can find six-figure or seven-figure sums to fund glitzy marketing campaigns, to make themselves feel good, but cannot find even a few thousands to conduct the market research that would tell them what customers really think and feel. Where market research is commissioned, the researchers are often prevented from asking any really pertinent questions on the grounds that it will upset the customers or that 'we already know the answers'. Or the questionnaire is unconsciously designed to elicit the kind of answers that will enable the board to continue living in cloud-cuckoo-land.

In other organisations, corporate amnesia is expressed in the form of an excessively zealous concentration on factors such as quality control, personnel relations or manufacturing techniques. These displacement activities are there to reassure the corporate unconscious that success is not the arbitrary result of chance but that the factors affecting success are under the corporation's rational control.

The beginning of healthy behaviour for most corporations is to confront and acknowledge the chaos-related nature of the markets in which they work and the fortuitous nature of their initial success; and by this means to seek to put themselves in a position to be opportunistic again. In order to repeat their earlier successes, corporations must learn to become the hungry opportunists once more that they were when they were young. They must devote their R and D expenditure to positioning themselves to once again engage opportunely with future markets as they develop and open. This in turn implies backing as many innovations as is practical in order to be there when the next wave comes.

This prescription will not be welcome news to many companies. It is a tall order for most of them. But there is no other way for them to stay in the game, other than to continue to do what has worked in the past, and hope that it will continue to work in the future.

Alfred P Sloan, legendary president of General Motors from 1923 to 1946 during the period of its emergence as a dominant force in the car industry, summarised his experience as follows: 'It is not easy to say why one management is successful and another is not. The causes of success or failure are deep and complex, and chance plays a part. Experience has convinced me however, that for those who are responsible for a business, two important factors are motivation and opportunity. The former is supplied in good part by incentive compensation, the latter by decentralisation.'[1]

Sloan was writing in 1963. Perhaps today we might add that decentralisation is a necessary precursor to creating opportunity, but the clarity of vision that can come only from a healthy mind is equally essential to grasping that opportunity and hence to success in the long term.

CHAPTER EIGHTEEN

X-RAY VISION
How companies see the future

When x-rays were discovered by Wilhelm Roentgen in 1895, many members of the public were outraged. Misunderstanding the scientific implications of the new discovery, the corseted Victorians feared that anyone who equipped themselves with x-ray spectacles would be free to see whatever they wished – through walls, through houses, inside locked drawers, and even through clothes. Privacy, they believed, would be at an end. Their fears, of course, were misplaced. Though a powerful tool, x-rays could not be used to indulge such a perverse appetite for spying.

Ironically, a century later, the growth of Internet technology is having almost the opposite effect on people's perceptions. In the information age, when the most intimate secrets are available every morning in the tabloid press, people see electronic communications as a *more* secure way of communicating: a way of concealing their intimate thoughts and plans. Yet the Internet has done in practice what x-rays did only in our grandfather's imagination: provided an instrument of observation to which there are no effective barriers.

A common theme of many of the case histories examined in this book is the dramatic effect that increased availability of information, through electronic communications, has had on companies of all kinds. In essence, the effect is comparable to the players in a game of poker being compelled to play with their cards on the table. When bluffing is no longer an option, entirely new strategies are called for if a player wants to stay in the game.

I predict that within a matter of decades, and not many decades at that, few of the companies written about in this book will continue to exist in their present form. In one sense this is not such a dramatic prediction as it may seem. *The Times* first published a list of Britain's 300 top industrial companies in 1965. Only 32 companies out of that original top 100 are still in the top 100 today. The picture is much the same in the United States where almost half the companies listed in the 'Fortune 500' – 230 companies – disappeared from the list in the 1980s alone. Even more striking is the fact that of the 100 largest US corporations in 1900, only 16 are still even in existence.

My reason for making such a far-reaching prediction, however, is more than merely the tide of history that wears away all but the most durable of foundations. It is that there are a number of important new social forces acting to break up or radically alter the present structure of large companies; forces whose effects are already beginning to be felt.

The first and most important of these is the easy availability of information. Even while companies like BNFL and Marlboro protest that nuclear energy and tobacco are safe, we have the information on our home PCs that shows the real facts. At some point in the near future it will no longer be necessary to fight a lengthy and protracted court case over this or other issues, because investors, consumers, regulators and employees will accept the conclusions of properly conducted debates on the Internet and vote with their feet or their cheque books. No one will be listening any longer to empty assertions.

One outcome of the Global Village is that truth will be re-established. There will be a commonality of viewpoint that was unattainable with the multiplicity and diversity of information sources in the past, each with their own hidden agenda, and their own 'spin' on the facts. Instead of this fragmentation and dissonance there will be integration and unity of fact; there will again be such a thing as truth, publicly available truth, which can form the basis of informed decisions.

The lesson of the Shell Brent Spar affair is that ordinary customers can and will exercise choices that express their disapproval of suppliers' behaviour based on accurate, unbiased information. More and more people will choose to exercise the power that their purchasing confers on them as a matter of social conscience, based on their access to such information.

Another major source of pressure for change comes from the area of regulation. One of the important ways in which the corporate regulatory environment is set to change in future is regarding just what companies will and will not be permitted to say about their products and other people's.

When I became a journalist as a youngster in the 1960s, it was inconceivable that a government minister or senior civil servant could tell a blatant lie as a matter of policy. Broadly speaking, large corporations were also seen, and reported, as being basically honourable. This may well have been a naïve belief but it was one shared by the majority of people. Certainly, no newspaper would ever have published such an accusation in the 1960s. Yet when the Cabinet Secretary, Sir Robert Armstrong (now Lord Armstrong), the most senior civil servant in Britain, admitted misleading a court of law in 1987, the chief point of interest seemed to be his amusingly quaint choice of words – he said he had been 'economical with the truth'.[1] Much the same thing applied five years later when government minister Alan Clark described lying about government policy on arms as 'being economical with the *actualité*'.[2]

It is not the moral consequences of this kind of thing that concerns us here. It is the social consequences, which may be even worse than the effects of pumping chemical pollutants into the oceans and the atmosphere.

Organisations have sown the seeds of a new form of pollution that could be far worse in its effects on our children than any industrial pollution: that of information pollution. The uncontrolled dissemination of lies, half-truths, propaganda, 'spin' and disinformation by commercial companies, institutions, politicians and governments for reasons of policy and personal gain, may prove infinitely more destructive.

Information pollution seeps constantly out of organisations of almost all kinds into the river of social life. Moral stature is no protection against being a polluter: the Vatican, the Church of England and practically every other organisation, whether their aims are good or ill, sometimes use information pollution as an instrument of policy without realising the long-term consequences. Untruths, half-truths and weasel words are disseminated through newspapers and magazines, radio and television, cinema, books and a hundred minor information tributaries. Ultimately it comes to rest in the human mind where it becomes our oral culture and in libraries where it becomes our history. It becomes lodged in the organs of society and often remains permanently. Its effects are thus cumulative, just like lead poisoning or ozone layer depletion.

Just as no one knew what was the critical level of lead pollution or ozone depletion, because it had never before been experienced, so no one today knows what is the critical level of information pollution and what the likely consequences of exceeding that critical level will be. But it does not take much imagination to see the kind of result that might follow if the human mind and human libraries contained more false information than true, and people began to act on that false information.

The most striking recent example of such official misinformation having potentially devastating effects is the affair of BSE in cattle and the Government's repeated scientific assurances that beef was safe because BSE was not transmissible to humans. The 60 million inhabitants of Britain are still waiting to learn just how many of them are going to die because of the fatal inaccuracy of these assurances.

Regulators are closing in on corporations from several directions, but one of the most important is in circumscribing what companies can say about themselves and about their products and services. It is *already* a statutory offence for a publicly quoted company to lie about its financial prospects or the ingredients of the products it sells.

Within the next decade, these statutory safeguards are likely to be expanded considerably, so that many of the examples of deception described in earlier chapters become an offence, either against consumer protection legislation or against industry watchdog standards.

Another source of fundamental change is that, in many, perhaps most markets, size of organisation is no longer equated with strength, or perceived as a source of strength. At almost any time since the turn of the last century, size has been a corporate asset: it has been used very effectively to reassure customers about integrity; quality of product or service; continuity; financial stability; excellence of treatment for staff, wholesale and retail distribution channels and, ultimately, the customer. The marketing paradigm centred on the strength and security that springs from great size: the model of Hercules or Atlas – wise and just, as well as strong.

Over the last two decades this perception has undergone a radical shift. Now small is beautiful. Large organisations are suspect. Big Brother is watching you. The bigger the bureaucracy the more scope for incompetence, scapegoating and buck passing. Few people any longer equate size with quality; indeed there is a distinct trend towards smaller, more flexible organisations and especially towards the single individual providing specialist services economically and with accountability.

This trend is most visible at present in specialist services such as marketing, public relations, graphics design, advertising, engineering design and computer software. Here, even the largest corporations look for and expect better service than from someone like themselves. This trend, fuelled by the emergence of low-cost computer and communications technologies, is driving the teleworking revolution. And it is the best and the brightest individuals who are breaking away from the big corporations and setting up shop on their kitchen tables: often it's the dead wood that is left behind.

In the past, when large companies have been faced with social change, they have been able to adapt their organisations to that change. When people became tired of frozen roast beef and demanded more adventurous food, supermarkets adapted by giving them frozen stir-fry. Indeed, one way of looking at those companies was as commercial mechanisms that could be re-tuned to reflect current tastes.

But the social changes implied by the developments described in this book are not changes to which organisations can adapt and still maintain their present stance or even their present form. Fine tuning won't do it.

If it is fundamental to a company's culture to keep secrets, then how will it adapt to the see-through society? If it is fundamental to a company to dictate its customers' tastes, then how will it respond to customers' discovery of their power to dictate to suppliers? If a company manages its hold on its customers by telling lies, what will it do or say when its customers have discovered the truth, and corporate lies – even little white ones – are made illegal?

In these changing circumstances, the centre of gravity in the commercial equation is shifting radically towards the consumer's end rather than the supplier's end and the leverage will end up with the consumer. The conscious power of customers will become sufficiently great that companies will become no more than interpreters of public demand: like the out-of-town warehouses that exist to stack the boxes high and pass credit cards through their tills.

In the past there has been a fundamental inequality in the market transaction between vendor and customer; an inequality or advantage on the part of the vendor that has justified the vendor's margin and that, so to speak, represents the vendor's advantage in the tangible form of profits. This advantage or inequality takes many forms: the greater knowledge and skill of the coffee importer; the higher technical prowess of the personal computer manufacturer; the bulk-buying power of the supermarket.

But the fundamental basis of these inequalities is being eroded from the supplier–customer relationship by a levelling process represented by the social trends described earlier.

Technological skill is no longer provided by engineering staff: it comes packaged in a silicon chip and is ordered from the catalogues of Intel or Texas Instruments. Technical or marketing information is no longer a marketable commodity: it is free on the Internet. There is nothing magic about buying Columbian or Jamaican coffee beans: the magic is in the freeze-drying plant that anyone can buy or rent. Perhaps the only marketing differential that will continue to exist will be wholesale purchasing power and even here, the corporations are already cutting each other's throats to deliver the lowest prices possible. At the moment, for instance, cans of baked beans are being traded at three pence – one-tenth their normal price – by many of the major supermarket chains as part of a price war. It is impossible to conceive of this happening twenty, ten or even five years ago. Something is changing. A tacit consensus has broken up under increasing pressure of market competition, just as the

Antarctic ice-shelf is breaking up due to global warming: things cannot be put back the way they were.

Another exception will be companies who are innovators in technology, who will still be able to dictate for a time to their markets as the sole source of their innovations. But few of the major companies mentioned in this book come in that category. McDonald's, Coca-Cola, Shell, Ford, IBM, the high street banks, the brewers, the supermarkets, the drug companies – none of them is truly an innovator. They are simply bigger than their competitors and own a large slice of the market, or survive on their financial muscle. In financial and commercial terms they *are* the continental ice-shelf that is breaking up.

Most crucial of all in this new environment, which is so inimical to everything that large corporations traditionally stand for, it is the big companies who are least well-equipped to cope. All the factors that have contributed to the building up of large monolithic organisations, with unscalable walls and shock-proof public relations battlements, are the same factors that will make them unable to cope with the markets of the twenty-first century. The safety in numbers syndrome; the pull up the drawbridge tendency; the corporate PR game to deflect criticism and blame; the anonymity – all these are attitudes and postures that are inimical to survival in an environment that calls above all for tactical flexibility, flair and audacity – *an organisation of the imagination.*

The future for many of today's largest organisations is one of becoming more vulnerable and more beleaguered with each year that passes, like mediaeval castles in a hostile landscape, clung onto stubbornly by their defenders beyond all reason until the realisation finally dawns that the real world has moved on, and that the army besieging them no longer consists of armoured knights with siege engines, but of men and women who will conduct the business of the future, working at home with a PC, a modem and a telephone.

What should we, their customers, shareholders, employees, do about bad companies? Should we form protest groups? Lobby our politicians to enact legislation curbing the corporate appetite? Take to the streets with placards – or even house bricks?

None of these actions is necessary. All that is needed to bring large corporations to heel is simply for us to make our feelings and our wishes known by translating them into rationally directed buying policies, as Shell's customers did – by spending our money with companies that take care not to behave antisocially, and refusing to support bad companies.

This in turn raises the question: how can we reliably tell which companies are bad and which are good? Which are worth supporting with our custom and which should be avoided?

CHAPTER NINETEEN

WANTED FOR QUESTIONING
Corporate psychological profiling

In the days of the Wild West, it was easy to tell the bad guys from the good guys simply by reading the 'Wanted' posters. Today, telling the bad companies from the good companies is not so easy: on the outside, they all look very much the same.

As customers, shareholders or suppliers, or even prospective employees, we need some rule of thumb to enable us to gauge the mental health and likely behaviour of the companies and other organisations with whom we come in contact. Can the company be trusted? Does it speak the truth? Will it deal fairly and honestly with us in its transactions? Will it keep its word? And, perhaps most importantly, how will it behave when the chips are down? If the organisation were an individual, is it the kind of person you would go mountain-climbing with, or exploring in the jungle?

One difficulty with identifying the corporate state of mind with any accuracy is that, like individuals, sick companies often appear perfectly normal. Just as the psychopathic individual has learned to blend into the background by imitating his healthy peers, so the psychopathic company can pass most casual inspections as unremarkable.

Police organisations such as Scotland Yard and the Federal Bureau of Investigation have developed the technique of psychological profiling, to help them identify psychopathic offenders who might otherwise avoid scrutiny and escape detection. Anyone interested in analysing the mental health of corporations and other institutions can make use of similar techniques to determine just how reliable and trustworthy companies are. The following notes are a do-it-yourself guide to compiling a psychological profile of a company or other organisation.

The first essential step is to define what constitutes a healthy corporation. In the light of the issues discussed in this book, a useful working definition is that a healthy organisation is one that:

* Sees itself clearly

* Sees its customers clearly

* Portrays itself truthfully

* Deals openly and honestly with criticism

* Treats its employees fairly

* Shows no obvious signs of irrational behaviour

* Does not handicap itself unconsciously

* Is not afraid to innovate or afraid to fail

* Does not owe its success to factors beyond its control

* Is not trying to repeat the past instead of facing the future, but is managed rationally and efficiently.

Anyone can get a fair idea of these ten key diagnostic criteria of psychological health simply by looking systematically at the clues that organisations provide in their everyday behaviour – the things they say; the things they do; the products or services they market; the actions and attitudes of the people who work for them – and by interpreting those signs in the light of the unconscious factors discussed in this book.

The following is a checklist of diagnostic criteria for telling the healthy organisation from the unhealthy. The suggested points scoring system is a simple way of quantifying each of the criteria and hence of getting some idea of how, overall, a corporation shapes up in comparison with its peers.

There are many sources of corporate and institutional data that can be searched for the answers to these diagnostic questions. Probably the easiest source is the Internet since, today, every commercial company and other institution has a web site that, typically, publishes an annual report and recent press releases. It is, of course, still possible to obtain a copy of practically any company's annual report by writing or telephoning its public relations department to ask for a copy. Alternatively, the Department of Trade and Industry has a commercial library which is open to everyone and which contains copies of most annual reports and other information.

How Does the Organisation See Itself?

We're not, of course, interested in the company's conscious estimate of itself – the kind of guff talked in its press releases and annual report – except in so far as those PR statements can occasionally provide unconscious clues to the company's real nature and motives. What we are looking for are obvious signs of self-delusion.

The tell-tale signs here include the impossible promises in corporate mission statements ('Our goal is total customer satisfaction' and the like) and the phoney, meaningless corporate slogans ('When all you want is everything', 'Whatever it takes'), and other such drivel.

Of course, the fact that a company has fallen victim to this kind of marketing-speak doesn't mean that it believes these statements or even necessarily that it has gone to the bad. But it does show clearly that the organisation's board is careless of its corporate image and has allowed it to fall into the hands of outsiders. This is a warning signal of a self-deluding company: if they are willing to buy into these superficial slogans, then they no longer have a firm grasp on who they are and what they do. They have begun to confuse images with reality. And they are weak-minded enough to be dazzled by clever words.

Score 10 points if the company has a 'mission statement', and an additional 10 points if it uses a corporate slogan on its advertising or as part of its corporate livery. Score a further 10 if either or both of the statements are obvious nonsense or laughable.

How Does the Organisation See its Customers?

The annual report tells you a great deal about how the organisation sees its customers and its shareholders. Is the report frankly informative even about the bad things? Or is it full of weasel-worded evasions and attempts to gloss over bad news?

Does it leave out entirely the things the company does not want its shareholders and customers to know about? Even worse, is the company trying to cover up such matters by claiming they cannot be talked about because they are 'subject to legal action' (this is almost never true)? If the corporation has adopted any of these 'information management' strategies rather than an open approach, it means that the company sees its shareholders, customers – and even its own staff – as *outsiders* who can't be trusted to make up their own minds on the facts.

Make a comparison of the problems the company has encountered during the year as reported in the press and as they themselves have reported them to the financial community. Have they grasped the nettle, come clean and told their shareholders about the marketing failures, the redundancies, the dangerous products that had to be recalled? Or have the nastier events been wrapped up in weasel words and hidden away in an inconspicuous corner?

If it's the latter, then the chances are the company is afraid to tell the truth because it is afraid of how we will react when we know the truth, unless they have pre-digested it for us. This is not a basis for an equitable relationship. It is another warning signal of dangerous personality weaknesses. Score 10 points for every major black mark that is glossed over and 20 points for any that are omitted entirely. Score another 10 if the omission is claimed to be 'for legal reasons'.

How Does the Company Portray Itself?

Take a close look at the organisation's advertisements and ask: what are they really saying? Are they trying to make people believe things that simply aren't true – perhaps things that the organisation merely *wishes* were true? Are they trying to depict what The *Independent* called a 'rosy and uncomplicated picture', and if so, then why *exactly*?

It is not pathological for the company to seek to make a legitimate profit and to indulge in a little creative exaggeration to help it along. But if the content of its advertisements is the opposite of the truth, then something is deeply wrong. Car exhausts do not make pretty flowers grow on the roadside: they poison the environment. So why do some car manufacturers seek to show in their advertisements that their vehicles have this beneficial affect? The only explanation can be deception. A company that thinks it can con its customers like this, thinks it can con anyone about practically anything: it is not an organisation that can be trusted to think straight.

In many cases, the organisation and its agency realise that it would be going too far actually to claim the opposite of the truth. It would, for example, be laughable today to claim in print that smoking was good for your health (as some tobacco advertisements attempted to do in the 1950s) because this would be perceived immediately as a lie. In such cases, companies sometimes merely attempt to show the lie rather than tell it directly, for example by showing a healthy-looking cowboy enjoying a cigarette in beautiful open country, or – now that the cowboy has died of lung cancer – simply the beautiful countryside.

Score 10 points for every attempt to deceive by stating, or showing, the *opposite* of the truth.

How Does the Company Deal With its Critics?

Every large organisation has critics amongst environmentalists, consumers and other organisations and individuals with grievances. Do they respond openly to such critics, meeting them with honest, open debate? Or do they refuse to acknowledge and deal with external criticism, resorting to the usual PR formula of soft-soap, denials and rationalisations? Worst of all, do they attempt to squash debate about their commercial practices by threats of litigation or actually resorting to the law?

If a company has ever issued writs for libel against national newspapers or television companies, or repeatedly done so against private individuals such as environmentalists or consumerists, this is a very significant sign of something seriously wrong. Regardless of the outcome of any such litigation, always treat a company that resorts to libel litigation with deep suspicion.

Do not be overly concerned simply because a company is made the subject of an adverse report by newspapers or television. Reporters are often approached by people who believe they have been wronged or believe that a company is behaving irresponsibly. It is the function of the press to investigate allegations of this kind – they make good stories – and being bad-mouthed by the press is part of the price of being in the public eye. There is only cause for concern if the company clams up, refuses to comment, or threatens the media for doing its job.

Score 50 points for every libel writ issued by the company. Score 20 points for every important occasion on which the company refuses to participate in or comment on an investigative film or story. Score nothing for merely being written about or featured on TV in a bad light, if the company defends itself rationally.

How Does the Company Treat its Employees?

Most large organisations observe good form, at least outwardly, when it comes to treating their employees well, because they are acutely aware of the possible consequence of failing to, so don't expect to find any obvious signs of maltreatment. Just as companies no longer send small boys up chimneys or work pit ponies to death, neither are they deliberately careless of safety or welfare issues in their clean, comfortable, well-lit offices.

A bad record of industrial relations is not by itself cause for concern because permanent bickering is sometimes the most effective method of survival for both management and staff – as used to be the case in mining and car manufacturing for instance. However, a record of strikes is a sign of deeper trouble.

A sign of an even deeper malaise is where there is serious industrial unrest and strikes in third world countries in which the company operates. Workers in such countries are so ill-protected and unemployment is usually so high that striking is a sign of desperate measures. If a company is behaving badly to workers in the third world, it will often try to excuse its behaviour by claiming that it is the local conditions that produce such a state of affairs, rather than the company's policies. The truth is that if British workers were without a century of legislative protection, then the company would treat them the same way as it treats its workers in Nigeria or Guatemala.

You can find out about industrial relations both at home and abroad by contacting the half dozen or so biggest unions who will have prepared literature on the company if it is a persistent offender.

Score 10 points for every strike at home and 50 points for every strike in a third world country.

Does the Company Show Signs of Irrational Behaviour?

This is by no means easy to spot but is made easier by the knowledge that such behaviour is possible. In the past, episodes such as those described in previous chapters were regarded simply as errors of judgement or marketing mistakes, rather than seen as outbursts of disturbed behaviour caused by unconscious motivations.

The thing to look for here is the unaccountable. If the company has made a major investment decision that is inexplicable in terms of normal business practices, that decision should be examined with extra care to see if it is not simply an example of irrational behaviour. There are several common tell-tale signs that something is wrong. One is when the company is behaving in a way that is in opposition to the course of action that most rational outside observers expect it to take. Another is when the organisation digs in its heels and stubbornly refuses to reconsider its position, even when most outside observers consider that it is foolish or self-defeating for it to persist in its chosen course.

Care must obviously be taken not to attribute irrationality to actions that are merely imaginative, innovative or unconventional. No organisation should be penalised merely for attempting new goals or using new methods of achieving them.

Score 50 points for each example of undoubted irrational behaviour.

Is the Company Afraid to Innovate or Afraid to Fail?

How good is the company at picking winning products or services? Or at seeing what customers want and anticipating demand? How many successful new products has it introduced in the past year or two? And how many serious turkeys?

Innovation is a tightrope and companies can fall either side. If they are chronically bad at growing or finding successful new products, then their future is bleak. This is especially true if large amounts of their revenue are being swallowed up in research and development investment that is not paying off. On the other hand, the company's future is equally bleak if it is continually innovating and continually failing to find a winner – once again made worse if R and D spending is excessive.

This 'innovation tightrope' cannot be quantified simplistically but a rough guide is as follows. If a company is spending more than 10 per cent of its revenue on research and development, then it should also be regularly innovating products that are capable of contributing substantially to profitability for a reasonable time (more than a year, say). If it is persistently innovating but the new products do not meet these criteria, then something has gone wrong. If it is spending this much on R and D and not innovating regularly, then something has gone wrong.

For failure to innovate significantly despite spending 10 per cent of revenue on R and D, score 20 points. For persistent failure of innovations despite spending 10 per cent of revenue on R and D, score 20 points.

Another important danger signal is excessive spending on marketing activities: advertising, public relations, direct mail, give-away gimmicks and the like. If the company is spending significantly more than 10 per cent of its revenue on marketing, then suspect the worst and look carefully to see if it is simply going on a spending spree to make itself feel good. For excessive marketing spending, score 20 points.

Is the Company Managed Efficiently?

In judging whether a company is managed efficiently, there is little to be learned merely from how financially successful it is. The key question is not: is the company financially successful? but rather: does the company owe its success to factors beyond its management's control? As discussed earlier, factors that actively stimulate management delusion can include: possession of a monopoly or near monopoly; an insatiable demand for the company's products or services; or having very low costs in relation to prices, for raw materials or labour.

The fact that a company enjoys a naturally high volume of sales and a high margin on those sales does not mean that its management is lazy or inefficient, but it does mean that the conditions are right for management inefficiency: it is therefore a useful warning signal of possible delusional corporate behaviour.

When evaluating what companies are really like, by all means examine the usual financial indicators, such as return on capital employed. But ask also how far the company conforms to the model described above. On a scale of 0 to 20, how much of a monopoly does the organisation have? On a scale of 0 to 20, how insatiable is the demand for its products or services? On a scale of 0 to 20, how high is the margin between what the organisation buys and what it sells? Convert your estimates directly to point scores. This last indicator can be tricky to estimate, especially for service organisations. Note especially that this is not synonymous with the company's reported profit margin.

How to Score

In general, the closer to zero a company scores, the healthier it is. Conversely, the higher its score, the more likely it is to be untrustworthy or otherwise a bad bet.

Remember that this is not a precision instrument, merely a rule-of-thumb means of gauging the level of selfishness a company exhibits and hence of telling whether it is nearer to the socially-friendly end of the spectrum or the socially-unfriendly end.

Weighting the results

Some allowance must be made for size and type of organisation. For example, the British Government employs so many people (more than 600,000) in so many different fields that it is bound to have many strikes each year (not to mention the fact that it is also a goldmine of examples of irrational behaviour).

It is thus advisable to consider multinational companies or very large organisations in smaller (perhaps country-sized or department-sized) units, except where their global activities are specifically in question (such as number of strikes in third world countries).

Less than 50 points

All companies are going to clock up a few unwelcome points at some time or other. A company that can score less than 50 or so is doing extremely well to remain relatively well-balanced and customer-friendly in such a tough, competitive, corporate environment. You can deal with this company with as much confidence as you would ever place in any commercial organisation.

50 to 100 points

This is probably where the majority of organisations are today, and is a reflection of how competitive trading conditions are, how little escapes the media's attention and how demanding we have become as consumers. Be a little wary of companies scoring in this range: don't believe what they say unless they can prove their words; don't part with any significant money for their products or services until you have investigated your intended purchases with extra thoroughness.

100 to 250 points

There are far too many companies in this category today; a fact that gives cause for concern. Companies in this category are untrustworthy too often in what they say and do; they are unlikely to stand behind their products or services to any serious extent if anything goes wrong; they will often try to weasel out of trouble unless they are compelled by the press or the courts to face up to the consequences of their actions. Deal with such companies only after exhaustive investigation or if you have a cast-iron contract. If you can get the same or similar product or service from another organisation with a lower point score, then do so. Deal only with companies in this group if you have no alternative or are able to satisfy yourself completely that the transaction will be to your benefit.

Put simply, make sure they can't gyp you, *before* parting with your money.

More than 250 points

Any company scoring significantly more than 250 is likely to have very serious problems and should be avoided completely. You cannot rely on this company at all and, even if its products or services are sound in themselves, they are being marketed at unacceptable cost to the community, so the organisation should not be encouraged to continue its present patterns of behaviour.

Spend your money elsewhere and help shorten the life – or change the behaviour – of these Bad Companies.

Answers to Corporate Slogan Quiz in Chapter Three

The corporate slogans belong to the following organisations

The Communications Specialists	(Dixons)
Lightening the Load	(Safeway)
The art of performance	(Jaguar)
Let's make things better	(Philips)
Food for Thought	(Magnet Kitchens)
We're here to help	(W H Smith)
More than just a bank	(NatWest)
Making life taste better	(Sainsbury's)
For ever for everyone	(National Trust)
When all you want is everything	(Hyundai)
How switched on can you get?	(Granada)
Driven by passion	(Fiat)
We care because you care	(Boots)
Whatever it takes	(Fedex)
In Tune with People	(Nationwide)

NOTES

Chapter One: *Jekyll and Hyde plc*

___

1. For Shell's own account of the Brent Spar affair, see: www.shell.com/uk-en/directory/0,4010,25268,00.html
2. For Greenpeace's account of its campaign, see the Greenpeace website at: www.greenpeace.org/~comms/brent/brent.html
3. Interviewed for BBC TV film, 'Shell and the Brent Spar', broadcast 1996
4. *ibid*
5. *ibid*
6. See Greenpeace press release, 'Greenpeace reveals leaked document: Brent Spar can be feasibly and cheaply decommissioned on land', dated 9 June 1995. The release can be read in full at: www.greenpeace.org/~comms/brent/june09.html

Chapter Two: *Figures in a Landscape*

___

1. A history of the Thalidomide affair is given in the judgement of the European Court of Human Rights on 'Sunday Times v United Kingdom'. The judgement can be read in full at: www.mediator.online.bg/eng/sundayt2.htm
2. See London School of Economics, Department of International Relations, *International Business in the International System*, chapter 12, at: www.aptn.org/ibis/chapt12.pdf
3. Ralph Nader, *Unsafe at Any Speed: The Designed-in Dangers of the American Automobile*, Grossman, New York, 1965

4. Speech delivered by Mr Ratner to the Annual Conference of the Institute of Directors in April 1991. See *Daily Mail* article at: www.thisismoney.com/20010201/nm27286.html

5. For historical background to Coca-Cola see: www.coca-cola.com/about/index.html and select the 'Historical timeline' feature

6. See Frederick Allen, *Secret Formula: How Brilliant Marketing and Relentless Salesmanship Made Coca-Cola the Best-Known Product in the World*, Harper Business, New York, 1995

7. See Robert Hartley, *Marketing Mistakes*, John Wiley, New York, 1995

Chapter Three: *Mirror, Mirror, on the Wall*

1. Robert Townsend, *Up the Organisation*, Michael Joseph, London, 1970

2. See, for example, *New Research Shows Global 'Footprint' of Motoring* at: www.foe.co.uk/pubsinfo/infoteam/pressrel/1996/19960606151456.html

3. A history of London Greenpeace (back to 1908) is given at: www.mcspotlight.org/people/biogs/london_grnpeace.html

4. The McDonald's libel case is charted at: www.mcspotlight.org/case/index.html

5. McDonald's website is at www.mcdonalds.com, although it carries no information regarding its libel litigation

6. See: www.mcspotlight.org/case/index.html

7. *ibid*

8. *ibid*

9. *ibid*

10. *ibid*

11. *ibid*

12. *ibid*

13. See *What a Judge Said About McDonald's*, by Patricia Wynn Davies, Legal Affairs Editor of the *Independent*, 20 June 1997. Read her article at:- www.mcspotlight.org/media/press/independ_20jun97.html

Chapter Four: *Little White Lies*

1. Friends of the Earth, 'Green Con of the Year Awards', 1989–91
2. *ibid*
3. *ibid*
4. *ibid*
5. See, Advertising Standards Authority website: www.asa.org.uk/issues/ (look under 'Environment')
6. The first ad was broadcast on ITV in 1991. Surprisingly, Kenco is still today (June 2001) claiming on its website that the character played by Miss Lunghi represents the new chief of Kenco itself. See: www.kraftfoods.co.uk/kenco/advertising.htm
7. ITC's Advertising Complaints Reports can be read at: www.itc.org.uk/ divisions/ad_spons/ad_complaints.html

Chapter Five: *Just a Tiny Mistake*

1. Kim Philby, *My Secret War*, London 1968
2. Curt Gentry, *J Edgar Hoover: The Man and the Secrets*, W W Norton and Co. New York, 2001
3. An interactive history of the microprocessor is given on Intel's site at: www.intel.com/intel/museum/25anniv/index.htm
4. See *Divided it Fails — Pentium Arithmetic Bug Angers Users*, PowerPC News, 2 December 1994. The article can be read online at: www.lri.fr/ archi/mirror/cic/archive/fdir_bug
5. *ibid*
6. *ibid*

Chapter Six: *Good and Faithful Servants*

1. Peter Wright, *Spycatcher: The Candid Autobiography of a Senior Intelligence Officer*, Viking, 1987.
2. *ibid*

3. *ibid*
4. See David Leigh, *Economical With the Truth: The Breakdown of Ministerial Responsibility*, Charter 88. The article can be read in full at: www.gn.apc.org/Charter88/pubs/violations/leigh.html

Chapter Seven: *Companies on the Couch*

1. Sigmund Freud, *Group Psychology*, (1921), W W Norton, 1955
2. Cartright and Zander, *Introduction to Group Dynamics*, 1968
3. Gustave Le Bon, *The Crowd: A Study of the Group Mind*, 1920
4. McDougall, *The Group Mind*, 1920
5. Gustave Le Bon, *The Crowd: A Study of the Group Mind*, 1920
6. Robert de Board, *The Psychoanalysis of Organisations*, Tavistock Institute, London, 1978
7. *ibid*
8. *ibid*
9. Adam Raphael, *Ultimate Risk: The Inside Story of the Lloyd's Catastrophe*, Four walls Eight Windows, New York, 1995
10. *ibid*
11. *ibid*
12. *ibid*
13. *ibid*
14. *ibid*
15. *ibid*

Chapter Eight: *It's My Party and I'll Cry if I Want To*

1. For IBM's historical background see: www.ibm.com/investor/index_ibmdata.phtml and select 'Trace history...'.
2. For press opinion on OS/2, see John C Dvorak writing in *PC Magazine Online*, August 1995, 'Note to IBM: Sell the OS/2 Division'. The article can be read at: www.zdnet.com/pcmag/issues/1414/pcm 00041.htm

3. For an analysis of IBM's mishandling of the market by an insider, see *The Rise and Fall of IBM*, by Jean-Jacques Duby, Scientific Director of UAP, former Science and Technology Director of IBM Europe, 1995. His report can be read at: www.ecole.org/report_ibm.htm
4. See Norman Dixon, *On the Psychology of Military Incompetence*, Jonathan Cape, London, 1976

Chapter Nine: *The Cruel World of Woolly Jumpers*

1. For corporate background on Benetton, see: www.benetton.com/investors/overview
2. Advertising Standards Authority 1991 adjudication following record numbers of complaints about Benetton's 'Baby' advertisement

Chapter Ten: *Go Home, Mickey Mouse*

1. 'Pandora's Box: The Engineers' Plot', written and produced by Adam Curtis, broadcast on BBC2, 1992
2. 'Pandora's Box: Goodbye Mrs Ant', written and produced by Adam Curtis, broadcast on BBC2, 1992
3. See Robert Hartley, *Marketing Mistakes*, John Wiley, New York, 1995
4. *ibid*

Chapter Eleven: *Not Invented Here*

1. See *Jane's International Defence Review*, April 1993
2. For an account of the *Tomorrow's World* broadcast and other tests, see *Business Week*, 16 August 1993, 'Plastic that Can Withstand a Nuclear Blast?'
3. For some updates on 'Starlite', see www.charm.net/~dmg/mysteries/mystery1.html

Chapter Twelve: *They Would Say That, Wouldn't They?*

1. Frederick Winterbotham, *The Ultra Secret*, London, 1979
2. Gordon Welchman, *The Hut Six Story*.
3. See 'Nuclear Power: Death Confirmed at 2pm, 11 December 1995': www.foe.co.uk/pubsinfo/infoteam/pressrel/1995/19951211181706.html
4. Leon Festinger, *A Theory of Cognitive Dissonance*, Stanford University Press, California, 1962
5. BNFL's annual report for 2000, together with reports on environment, health and safety, and radioactive discharges, can be downloaded from its website at: www.bnfl.co.uk/website.nsf/default.htm
6. See Lorna Arnold, *Windscale 1957*, Palgrave Press (Macmillan), London, 1995
7. *ibid*
8. *ibid*
9. *ibid*
10. *ibid*
11. BNFL 'Company Profile', 1995

Chapter Thirteen: *Put Not Your Trust in Princes*

1. Perrier's corporate history is given on its website at: www.ucad.fr/pubgb/virt/mp/perrier/
2. See Robert Hartley, *Marketing Mistakes*, John Wiley, New York, 1995
3. *ibid*
4. *ibid*

Chapter Fourteen: *The Shell Game*

1. Leon Festinger, Henry W Riecken and Stanley Schachter, *When Prophecy Fails: A Social and Psychological Study*, University of Minnesota Press, 1956
2. Hoover's UK company history is given at: www.hoover.co.uk

3. See Robert Hartley, *Marketing Mistakes*, John Wiley, New York, 1995
4. *ibid*

Chapter Fifteen: *Luck of the Devil*

---

1. For Barclays financial results, shareholder information and company background, see: www.investor.barclays.co.uk/

Chapter Seventeen: *A Suitable Case for Treatment*

---

1. Alfred P Sloan, *My Years with General Motors*, Doubleday, New York, 1964

Chapter Eighteen: *X-ray Vision*

---

1. See David Leigh, *Economical With the Truth: The Breakdown of Ministerial Responsibility*, Charter 88. The article can be read in full at: www.gn.apc.org/Charter88/pubs/violations/leigh.html
2. *ibid*

INDEX OF COMPANIES

RICHARD MILTON

DEAD SECRET

It was obvious from the day of his birth that the Gabriel boy took after his mother in every way. He would be a marked man from birth to death…

When Tony Gabriel's mother dies, the last thing he expects to inherit are the research papers and books of a famous historian, on Revolutionary France – and a human skull. With no clue to the meaning of this mysterious bequest, Tony puts his years as a journalist to use to begin an investigation – and is stunned by what he uncovers.

Suddenly, all the rules in his life seemed to have been broken at once.

Tony is bewildered by the horrifying conspiracy he begins to unravel. Can human heads really be used to predict the future of entire nations? Who would pay $7 million for the head of Leonid Brezhnev? Is the British government involved? Tony's inquisition leads him to The Chadwick Foundation – a wealthy institution whose bizarre beliefs both repel and attract him.

'You see more than ordinary people. It's in your blood.'

Tony's love affair with stunning, enigmatic, Evelyn Canning, keeper of The Foundation's secrets, turns his search for the truth into a very personal quest. Eve seems to know more about Tony than he knows about himself. Is he from an ordinary working-class background? Or descended from the Bourbon Kings and Queens of France – possessing inherited psychic gifts?

'Are you afraid of me?' she asked. 'Yes,' he said…
'Make them accept you – for my sake.'

When Tony is initiated into the ultimate terrifying secret, he has a decision to make that can cost him his life.

Once you know the secret – you're dead.

Internet: www.houseofstratus.com including author interviews, reviews, features.

Email: sales@houseofstratus.com please quote author, title and credit card details.

Order Line: UK: 0800 169 1780
USA: 1 800 509 9942
INTERNATIONAL: +44 (0) 20 7494 6400
                or +01 212 218 7649
(please quote author, title, and credit card details.)

Send to: House of Stratus Sales Department   House of Stratus Inc.
24c Old Burlington Street   Suite 210
London   1270 Avenue of the Americas
W1X 1RL   New York • NY 10020
UK   USA